The Bunker and W14 Productions
presents

T0190806

# WE ANCHOR
# IN HOPE

## By Anna Jordan

This production is kindly supported by
Arts Council England and the Carne Trust

The Bunker and W14 productions present WE ANCHOR IN HOPE in association with the Royal Court.

25 September – 19 October 2019.

This play was originally commissioned and produced by the Royal Court Theatre as part of the Beyond the Court programme.

## CAST, *in order of appearance*

| | |
|---|---|
| PEARL | Alex Jarrett |
| BILBO | Daniel Kendrick |
| FRANK | David Killick |
| SHAUN | Alan Turkington |
| KENNY | Valentine Hanson |

## CREATIVE TEAM

| | |
|---|---|
| Writer | Anna Jordan |
| Director | Chris Sonnex |
| Designer | Zoë Hurwitz |
| Lighting Designer | Jess Bernberg |
| Sound Designer | Emily Legg |
| Movement Director | Louise Kempton |
| Photographer | Helen Murray |
| Assistant Director | Rosemary Maltezos |
| Image | Tom Scurr and David Ralf |
| Videographer | Rosemary Maltezo |
| Production Manager | Zara Janmohamed |
| Producer | Annabel Williamson, W14 Productions |
| Stage Manager | Crystal Gayle |

## CAST (in order of appearance)

### ALEX JARRET | PEARL

Alex trained at The Brit School.

Alex's theatre credits include AISHA (Old Red Lion/King's Head/Tristan Bates) for which she received an Offie Nomination.

Her television credits include LES MISÉRABLES, THE REBEL, TRACEY BREAKS THE NEWS and THE JONAH MAN. She will appear as a regular in ADULT MATERIAL next year.

Radio includes MOLL FLANDERS and NICKED.

### DANIEL KENDRICK | BILBO

Daniel trained at Mountview Academy of Performing Arts.

Daniel's theatre credits include THE MONKEY and COALITION (Theatre503), FURY (Soho), SO HERE WE ARE (Royal Exchange/Hightide), OUR TOWN (Almeida), IF YOU DON'T LET US DREAM, WE WON'T LET YOU SLEEP, DING DONG THE WICKED and VERA, VERA, VERA (Royal Court), ROSIE AND JIM (Mobculture) and CHAPEL STREET (Liverpool Playhouse/Old Red Lion).

His film and television credits include #US AND THEM, OFFENDER, LOVE BITE, THE RIOT CLUB, CASUALTY, DAVE ALLEN AT PEACE, CALL THE MIDWIFE, BLACK MIRROR, RIPPER STREET, OUR WORLD WAR, MR. SELFRIDGE, RUN and EASTENDERS.

### DAVID KILLICK | FRANK

David's theatre credits include PRESSURE (Ambassadors), A ROOM WITH A VIEW (Theatre Royal Bath/tour), THE IMPORTANCE OF BEING EARNEST (West End/tour), THE CRUCIBLE and LIFE IS A DREAM (West Yorkshire Playhouse), A LITTLE HOTEL ON THE SIDE and THE SCHOOL FOR SCANDAL (Theatre Royal Bath), THE CAPTAIN OF KÖPENICK and HIS DARK MATERIALS (National Theatre), THE KING'S SPEECH (Wyndham's/ Yvonne Arnaud/tour), MEASURE FOR MEASURE and THE HYPOCHONDRIAC (Almeida), RESTORATION (Salisbury), FUNNY GIRL, THE MASTER AND MARGARITA and A MIDSUMMER NIGHT'S DREAM (Chichester), HEARTBREAK HOUSE (Watford Palace), SCENES FROM AN EXECUTION (Hackney Empire), SUMMER AND SMOKE (Nottingham Playhouse/West End), A MIDSUMMER NIGHT'S DREAM (RSC/City of London Sinfonia), AS YOU LIKE IT (Wyndham's), THE MADNESS OF GEORGE III (West Yorkshire Playhouse/ Birmingham Rep), CORIOLANUS and THE MERRY WIVES OF WINDSOR (RSC, Stratford/tour/Old Vic), THE WIND IN THE WILLOWS (Birmingham Rep), A SERVANT TO TWO MASTERS (RSC/ATG), RICHARD II, MEASURE FOR MEASURE, CORIOLANUS, PEER GYNT, LOVE'S LABOUR'S LOST, EDWARD II, THE COMEDY OF ERRORS, DON JUAN, HENRY IV PART 1 and 2, SARCOPHAGUS, MACBETH, WORLDS APART, ART OF SUCCESS, WASTE, THE DEVILS, A NEW WAY TO PAY OLD DEBTS, JULIUS CAESAR, THE LOVE GIRL and THE INNOCENT (RSC, Stratford/Barbican), CHARLEY'S AUNT (Crucible, Sheffield), RICHARD III (RSC/tour/Savoy), NEVERLAND (Royal Court), THE COUNTRY WIFE (Centreline Productions), HEDDA GABLER (ETT), A GOING CONCERN (Hampstead), TRANSLATIONS (Donmar Warehouse), A WOMAN OF NO IMPORTANCE (RSC/Barbican) and WHO'S AFRAID OF VIRGINIA WOOLF? (Royal Lyceum, Edinburgh).

His film and television credits include PRESSURE: D-DAY EVENT, SHAKESPEARE AND HATHAWAY, WITHOUT MOTIVE, MIDSOMER MURDERS, SHELLEY, ROUGH JUSTICE, THE BILL, TRUE TILDA, THE FAMOUS FIVE, MOVING STORY, A TOUCH OF FROST, NOT EVEN GOD IS WISE ENOUGH, LOVEJOY, THE HISTORY BOYS, MOJO, THE GROTESQUE and BYE BYE BABY.

Radio and voice work include THE JUDGMENT OF SHERLOCK HOLMES, DOCTOR WHO: THE LOST STORIES, PEARSON ELT – OUR DISCOVER ISLAND, POPTROPICA – ON THE FARM, BLITHE SPIRIT, MACBETH and MEASURE FOR MEASURE.

## ALAN TURKINGTON | SHAUN

Alan trained at the Royal Academy of Dramatic Art.

Alan's theatre credits include ANTONY AND CLEOPATRA (National Theatre), HAMLET (Donmar at Wyndham's Theatre/Elsinore Castle/Broadhurst Theatre, Broadway), A CRY FROM HEAVEN (Abbey), THE TEMPEST, THE WINTER'S TALE and PERICLES (RSC), IN THE BAR OF A TOKYO HOTEL (Charing Cross), GATES OF GOLD and JOHN FERGUSON (Finborough), JOHN BULL'S OTHER ISLAND (Tricycle), THE FIRST MAN and INFLAME (Jermyn Street), SWEET BIRD OF YOUTH (Dundee Rep), LAGAN (Ovalhouse), STARS IN THE MORNING SKY (Belgrade), A VIEW FROM THE BRIDGE (Harrogate), THE SANTALAND DIARIES (Union), TOUCH (Tristan Bates) and WHAT IF (Theatre Renegade/Southwark Playhouse).

His film credits include MARY QUEEN OF SCOTS, KING ARTHUR, DAD'S ARMY, NINE VOLTS, WANT IT, THE MAN FROM U.N.C.L.E., DRONE, IMPLEMENTATION, DOOR OUT OF THE DARK and PURE.

His television credits include MRS. WILSON, RELLIK, X COMPANY, MR. SELFRIDGE, STRIKE BACK, 10 DAYS TO WAR, HOLLYOAKS, SPYING ON HITLER'S ARMY, HOLBY CITY and DOCTORS.

Radio includes EIGHT HUNDRED AND THIRTY SEVEN POINT NINE, PORTRAIT OF A YEAR, JOURNEY FROM THE NEW WORLD and SOUL MUSIC.

Alan can also be heard introducing the programmes on Sky Atlantic.

**VALENTINE HANSON** I KENNY

Valentine's theatre credits include ORPHEUS DESCENDING (Theatr Clwyd/ Menier Chocolate Factory), HANDFAST (Summerhall, Edinburgh Festival), THE SISTERHOOD (Belgrade), HECTOR (Eden Court/Ambassadors), CUMING AND GOING (Bush), STOP SEARCH (Catford Broadway Studio), FOOTPRINTS IN THE SAND/LETTING GO/FOR ONE NIGHT ONLY (Pursued by a Bear), WORD PEACE: A CELEBRATION (Shakespeare's Globe), FESTEN and CAT ON A HOT TIN ROOF (Lyric), THE TEMPEST (Orange Tree), G.I. BLUES (Forest Forge Theatre Company), AFTER THE END OF THE WORLD (Red Ladder/national tour), POSITIVE MENTAL ATTITUDE (Theatre Centre/national tour) and THE ADVENTURES OF HUCKLEBERRY FINN (Classic Theatre/national tour).

His film and television credits include THE FRIDAY NIGHT PROJECT, MURDER CITY, LONDON VOODOO and CASUALTY.

# CREATIVE TEAM

### ANNA JORDAN | WRITER

Anna's recent plays include MOTHER COURAGE (Royal Exchange/Headlong), POP MUSIC (Paines Plough/Birmingham Repertory Theatre) and THE UNRETURNING (Frantic Assembly/Theatre Royal Plymouth). Anna won the Bruntwood Prize in 2013 for YEN. She was recently part of the writers room on HBO's BAFTA-winning series SUCCESSION, created by Jesse Armstrong, and has written episode 4, and is currently writing on the third series of KILLING EVE.

Anna has taught/directed at RADA, LAMDA, Arts Ed, Central and Italia Conti. She runs her own company, Without a Paddle Theatre, and co-founded Hackney Showroom Young Actors with Sam Curtis Lindsay. She is also the vocal coach for ALT Actor Training.

### CHRIS SONNEX | DIRECTOR

Chris is the Artistic Director of The Bunker and was previously Artistic Associate for the Royal Court. His credits include KATZENMUSIK and THE BOYS PROJECT: THE UNDERGROWTH (Royal Court Theatre Jerwood Theatre Upstairs), TOTTENHAM SYMPHONY, LINK UP and PIMLICO PLAYGROUND: RADIO PLAYS (Beyond The Court), TAKE THE STAGE (Donmar Warehouse Discover), REIMAGINING SUMMER & SMOKE & SUMMERVERSITY (Almeida Participation) and with Synergy Theatre Project HMP/ YOI Isis.

### ZOË HURWITZ | DESIGNER

Zoë is a Set Designer for stage and film based in London and New York. She is a graduate of New York University Tisch School of the Arts Masters Programme in Set Design and has a BA in Fine Art from Chelsea School of Art (University of the Arts London).

Theatre credits include TOMORROW WILL TAKE CARE OF ITSELF (NYU Tisch), SING GODDESS (Here Arts Centre NYC), THE XANDER XYST EXPERIENCE (Ars Nova NYC), FUCKING A (Yale School of Drama), LIE WITH ME (Talawa), LOVESONG OF THE ELECTRIC BEAR (The Hope/The Arts), THE BOYS UPSTAIRS (Above the Stag), UNCOMMON NONSENSE and PECKHAM THE SOAP OPERA (Royal Court).

## JESS BERNBERG | LIGHTING DESIGNER

Jess trained at Guildhall School of Music and Drama and was the 2018 Laboratory Associate Lighting Designer at Nuffield Southampton Theatres.

Designs include [BLANK] (Donmar Warehouse), ACTUALLY (Trafalgar Studios), A HISTORY OF SHOPPING MALLS IN TEHRAN (Traverse/Home MCR), RUST (Bush/HighTide), WONDROUS VULVA (Ovalhouse), OUT OF WATER and COUGAR (Orange Tree), THE CRUCIBLE, SEX SEX MEN MEN, A NEW AND BETTER YOU and BUGGY BABY (The Yard), THE TOWN THAT TREES BUILT (Young Vic), AND THE REST OF ME FLOATS (Birmingham Rep/Bush), THE BORROWERS (Tobacco Factory), FABRIC and DRIP FEED (Soho), VICTORIA'S KNICKERS and CONSENSUAL (NYT), MEDUSA, MUCH ADO ABOUT NOTHING, DUNGENESS and LOVE AND INFORMATION (Nuffield Southampton Theatres), HOMOS, OR EVERYONE IN AMERICA (Finborough), SONGLINES (HighTide), DEVIL WITH THE BLUE DRESS and FCUK'D (Off West End Award nomination) (Bunker).

Awards: 2017 Association of Lighting Designer's Francis Reid Award.


## EMILY LEGG | SOUND DESIGNER

Emily is Deputy Head of Sound at the Royal Court and produces the Royal Court Playwright's Podcast.

Theatre credits include HOLE, KATZENMUSIK, PLAQUES & TANGLES, YOUNG COURT SEASON, LIVE LUNCH, THE GET OUT, GASTRONAUTS and LOST IN THEATRE (Royal Court), TURNING A LITTLE FURTHER (Young Vic), CHECKPOINT 22 (New Diorama/Edinburgh Festival) and PEDRO PERAMO IS MY FATHER (Elan Frantoio).


## LOUISE KEMPTON | MOVEMENT DIRECTOR

Louise is a movement director, choreographer, intimacy co-ordinator, actor and puppeteer. She originally trained for her BA Hons in Acting at Rose Buford College and more recently at the Guildhall School of Music & Drama where she completed a masters in Movement.

Movement and choreography work includes RESURRECTING BOBBY AWL (Summerhall Edinburgh Fringe Festival), OUR COUNTRY'S GOOD (Tobacco Factory), CHAOS and TWELFTH NIGHT (Southwark Playhouse/National Theatre Connections), ARE THERE FEMALE GORILLAS? (Brighton Fringe), BOX CLEVER and KILLYMUCK (Bunker), THE NOISES (Old Red Lion), MUCH ADO ABOUT NOTHING (Merely Theatre) and THE LAST ONES (Ovalhouse).

Puppetry credits include WAR HORSE (National Theatre), THE SECRET GARDEN (Grosvenor Park Open Air Theatre) and ARIODANTE (Dutch National Opera). Movement direction for film includes NFST short PIGEONS.

Louise regularly teaches movement and acting classes at Guildhall School of Music & Drama, Northampton University and St Mary's University.

### ROSEMARY MALTEZOS | ASSISTANT DIRECTOR

Rosemary is a working-class director and designer from Swindon. She is a strong visual storyteller who wants theatre to be an honestly emotional, current and incredibly entertaining experience. Rosemary has just completed production on her first film, WARMER, a surreal exploration of loss and grief, which will be entering the festival circuit over the coming months. As a costume designer she specialises in performance art and dance and has an ongoing collaboration with performance artist Amelia Prett. In 2018 she also directed a successful run of WET (Theatre N16).

### ZARA JANMOHAMED | PRODUCTION MANAGER

Zara trained at the Royal Academy of Dramatic Art in Stage and Production Management.

Recent work has included: Production Management Edinburgh Fringe (Mick Perrin Worldwide), Shakespeare UK and European tour, RADA Festival, DRAMATIC DINING CABARET and ROTTERDAM (RADA), FUCK YOU PAY ME, BOX CLEVER/KILLYMUCK and GROTTY (Bunker), THE AMBER TRAP (Theatre503), HOARD, SITTING and MRS DALLOWAY (Arcola).

Stage Management: DICK WHITTINGTON AND HIS CAT and 80th ANNIVERSARY GALA (Oxford Playhouse), A PASSAGE TO INDIA (tour/Park), RAISING MARTHA and KILL ME NOW (Park) and SCAPEGOAT (St. Stevens Church).

### CRYSTAL GAYLE | STAGE MANAGER

Crystal trained at Essex University BA (Hons) Degree Technical Theatre.

Crystal's theatre credits include THE END OF HISTORY (Royal Court), INSIDE BITCH (Clean Break), SNOW WHITE AND SEVEN DWARFS (Regent), MYSTERIOUS GENTLEMAN (Courtyard), TREASURE ISLAND, MR TOD and RICHARD III (Red Rose Chain/The Avenue), THE TEMPEST, A MIDSUMMER NIGHT'S DREAM and THE COMEDY OF ERRORS (Red Rose Chain/Theatre in the Forest), ZATOPEK (Second Movement), COMMENCING (Joined At the Hip/Etcetera), A FACE IN A JAR (Inside Job Theatre Projects), BURIED CHILD (Ovation Theatre Limited), GAMBLING (Soho) and A VIEW FROM A BRIDGE (Mercury).

### ANNABEL WILLIAMSON | PRODUCER

Annabel Williamson is the founder of W14 Productions, focusing on new plays with a strong social conscience. Productions include BOX CLEVER/KILLYMUCK and 31 HOURS (Bunker), THE POLITICAL HISTORY OF SMACK AND CRACK (Edinburgh Fringe Festival/Soho/Mustard Tree), JAM (Finborough), THE BRINK (a co-production with the Orange Tree), THE LATE HENRY MOSS and UPPER CUT (Southwark Playhouse).

With four concrete pillars marking out a large thrust performance space, an eclectic mix of audience seating on three sides of the stage, and a craft beer bar, The Bunker is a visceral and unique performance space with a character of its own.

The Bunker believes in artists. We give ambitious artists a home in which to share their work with adventurous audiences. We are champions of each piece that we programme and we want to ensure our stage is filled with exciting, exhilarating, and contemporary theatre featuring artists that represent the world that we live in.

The Bunker was opened in October 2016 by founding directors Joshua McTaggart and Joel Fisher. The theatre's first year of work included the award-winning sell-out show SKIN A CAT and Cardboard Citizen's 25th Anniversary epic HOME TRUTHS. In-house productions have included festivals MY WHITE BEST FRIEND (and other letters left unsaid) and THIS IS BLACK as well as DEVIL WITH THE BLUE DRESS and the double bill KILLYMUCK & BOX CLEVER.

In September 2018, Artistic Director Chris Sonnex joined Executive Director David Ralf to lead the theatre's dedicated team, several of whom were involved in the original conversion of the space. Bunker Theatre Productions CIC is a not-for-profit theatre, which currently receives no public subsidy.

Find Out More
www.bunkertheatre.com
Box Office: 0207 234 0486
E-Mail: info@bunkertheatre.com
Address: 53a Southwark Street, London, SE1 1RU

## The Bunker Team

## THANKS

WE ANCHOR IN HOPE has been generously supported by
Arts Council England and The Carne Trust.

Thank you also to the Royal Court, the Gate Theatre, Guildhall
School of Music and Drama, Paines Plough, The Old Red Lion,
Ola Animashawun, Dan Brodie, Danny Brown, Aidan Carroll,
Rachel De-Lahay, Vicky Featherstone, Romana Flello, Grace
Gummer, Debbie Hannan, Aoife Lennon, Lucy Morrison, Hamish
Pirie, Rosie Stroud and Anoushka Warden without whose
support this production would not have been possible.

A special thanks to Asahi UK & The Meantime Brewery for all
their assistance in enabling us to transform The Bunker in to
The Anchor.

WE ANCHOR IN HOPE

Anna Jordan

*For Gryff, the boy.*
*When I wrote this you were just a dream.*

## A Note About this Play

*We Anchor in Hope* was commissioned by the Royal Court
Theatre as part of Beyond the Court in 2016. Chris Sonnex sent
me into pubs in Pimlico to buy drinks for people and talk to
them about their lives, their area and what pubs meant to them.
This play is a fictional piece in response to the many chats
I had with some fantastic and generous people. We performed
it as a rehearsed reading at a pub in Pimlico in 2016 and it has
been reworked for this, its premiere at The Bunker in 2019.
Cheers Pimlico.

*A.J.*

## Acknowledgements

Thank you to my dear friend Scott Le Crass – this play would not have been possible without him. Thanks to Darlene at LALGRA Community Hall and the people I chatted with at The Constitution and many other Pimlico pubs. Thank you to Peter Gordon, Alison King, David Hemsted, Young Sir Thomas Scurr, Hamish Pirie, Chris Urch, Camilla Young, Grace Gummer, Vicky Featherstone, Lucy Morrison, Jed O'Hagan, Adaleyo Adedayo, Colin Mace, Deka Walmsley, Katherine Kotz, Aoife Lennon, Jules Richardson. Thanks to David Eldridge for the advice. Thanks to the wonderful creatives, team, cast and fabulous teams at both The Bunker and the Royal Court. Huge love and thanks to the brilliant Annabel Williamson and huge love, adoration and gratitude to the irrepressible Chris Sonnex.

*A.J.*

## Characters

PEARL, *twenty, slim, tough, attractive, tomboyish*

BILBO, *twenty-four, scruffy and a little bit scrawny, a face that shows worries beyond his years*

FRANK, *seventy-seven, a touch of tired class about him. His vowels are RP but he occasionally drops his 'T's and 'H's*

SHAUN, *fifty, Northern Irish, athletic figure, strong shoulders, suntanned and weather-beaten from years of work outside. Ruggedly handsome*

KENNY, *fifty, the look of someone who's not been sleeping well*

## Note on Text

*/ indicates an overlap*

*/ at the end of a line indicates coming in very sharply on cue – almost overlapping*

*… denotes a trailing-off of thought rather than a slowing of pace*

*This text went to press before the end of rehearsals and so may differ slightly from the play as performed.*

## ACT ONE

*Late summer 2016. A dark and empty pub. It's an absolute shit
state – the debris of last night not cleared up yet: glasses, crisp
packets, a couple of stalls turned over, a rather deflated blow-
up sheep in the corner. There are also some paper plates with
some remnants of a buffet, the odd stray Wotsit, a lone sausage
roll lies under a chair. During the early sections the pub is
tidied and put in order. There's always something to do. For
now, there is just the hum of the fridges. It's a bit spooky.
PEARL enters. Dressed in trackie bottoms, a crop top and
jacket. She switches the light on. Looks at the mess.*

PEARL. Oh what??

*She takes her jacket off. She opens the back door, which
leads up to the flat and down to the cellar, and calls.*

LADS!

Kenny! Bill?

*She listens.*

*Nothing. She looks out over the pub. Quietly:*

Taking the fucking piss.

*She goes into a corner to collect glasses. The corner is
spotlit momentarily. She speaks to the audience. The memory
is fleeting but vivid and the text is delivered with rhythm
and pace.*

Late summer. 2003. Mum; hoop earrings and a G&T. Shaggy
on the jukebox: 'It Wasn't Me'. Patches of sweat under the
arms of her top. Well, it is fucking hot. Feels like summer
got fat and it's about to burst. We're coming back from
Nanny's but we've popped in here first.

Mum *basks* in the weight of the male gaze. Laughing. Posing. Pouting. Smoking; working her looks. And I'm in the corner with an ice pop and Disney Princess colouring book. I want hair down to my bum and a tiny waist – like Mum. What I've got is puppy fat and a lopsided bob that Auntie Shell did after seven pints.

Mum's with a boyfriend. Ricky, or Webster, or Steve? Yep, it's Steve, defo. Looking like the cat that got the cream. Back rod-straight, hackles up, he scans the pub. Does these jerky movements with his chin. Wants everyone to know that Fi's with *him*. He's set to pride for his first four drinks. Fifth one turns the dial to jealous rage.

My ice pop's melted on the page and my lips are blue. I've had jelly sweets at Nanny's too and I'm coming down off a sugar high. I want to go home. And sit on Mum's bed; copy her as she takes off her make-up and puts on all her creams and goo. It's my favourite thing to do. Princess Jasmine's got nothing on my mum. She shits all over Mulan and Belle. But Steve's coming back with us – I can tell. There's a sheen of sweat on the both of them. He hooks spindly fingers under bra straps, creeps them up her skirt like tarantula's legs. Her lips are parted, he whispers something in her ear and she throws her head back and laughs.

*She moves so she is not visible to* BILBO, *who enters from the stairs and floats around the bar area.*

I'm six. But already I think – what does it feel like when a man touches you?

*She gets lost in the thought.* BILBO *looks mournfully at the pub – then suddenly and spontaneously shouts into the empty space:*

BILBO. CHEL-SEE-/EEEEA!

PEARL. Fucking HELL, Bilbo!

BILBO. Oh my God!

PEARL. Idiot, man!                    BILBO. You scared me!

PEARL. You scared *me*, you twat.

BILBO. What you doing here?

PEARL. What does it look like, dick-face? I'm cleaning up!

BILBO. Why?

PEARL. Cos you didn't do it last night!

BILBO. I mean why bother? Let the brewery do it!

*He grabs an abandoned plate of food and chucks it over the floor.*

PEARL. KEN'S OPENING UP. Tonight.

*Beat. Confused.*

BILBO. I thought he weren't gonna bother.

PEARL. 'Business as usual. One more night. Do me proud.' Check your phone.

BILBO. Why would he text me? He lives with me.

*She looks at him. He checks it.*

Oh yeah.

PEARL. BILL. MOVE YOURSELF.

*PEARL goes back to tidying, BILBO helps.*

BILBO. He ain't come out of his room all day.

PEARL. Hungover.

BILBO. I left a latte and a sausage sandwich outside his door. 'S still there.

*Beat. PEARL works on.*

I would have thought he was fucking dead if he hadn't left a massive floater in the toilet.

PEARL. BILL!

BILBO. Sorry. But it was like an arm reaching for me.

*He shudders with the memory.* PEARL*'s phone rings: Amy Winehouse – 'Rehab'. She checks it and rejects it quickly.*

PEARL. You're a mug. You hungover?

BILBO. Nah I'm alright. I was sick.

PEARL. It was a good night. Loads of people we haven't seen for ages.

BILBO. Yeah.

PEARL. Can't believe Cathy Morris has got a new face.

BILBO. Yeah.

PEARL. They paid for it with their PPI. Tony must wake up every morning and be like WHO THE FUCK ARE YOU?

BILBO. *Tony* should get a new face. He looks like Mr Burns.

PEARL. Ha. Calvin was a knob.

BILBO. Coked up.

PEARL. Ken tried to bar him. And Calvin was like 'You're closing tomorrow, you clown!'

BILBO. Bet he loved that.

PEARL. Do you think he enjoyed it?

BILBO. Calvin?

PEARL. Ken, you muppet.

BILBO. Hard to tell. I think…

PEARL. What?

*Beat.*

BILBO. I think he's just. Really. Fucking. Gutted, Pearl, you know?

*They stop a moment.* PEARL *nods.*

You?

PEARL. Yeah. It's my job.

BILBO. Me too.

PEARL. But there'll be other jobs.

BILBO. Yeah. Still… shit though, innit?

PEARL. Shit happens. (*Carries on.*) We got one more night –
let's make it a good one for Ken.

*Beat.* BILBO *watches her.*

BILBO. I don't really know… what I'm gonna do.

PEARL. How d'you mean?

BILBO. Where I'm gonna go. Like.

PEARL. What about the Brixton place?

BILBO. Fell through.

PEARL. The studio flat?

BILBO. Yeah… The bloke fucked me over.

PEARL. How?

BILBO. Just did.

*Beat.*

PEARL. Bill, have you been telling porkies?

BILBO. No!

PEARL. 'Exaggerated' a bit?

BILBO. Look! People kept asking me, right, 'What you gonna
do, Bill?' 'Where you gonna go, Bill?' so I… said some things.

PEARL. Why?

BILBO. I thought it was gonna be alright. Thought this was
just… another 'blip'.

PEARL. This ain't no blip, babes.

BILBO. '*The bastards'll have to carry me out of this pub in my
coffin.*' Ken says.

PEARL. Ken didn't know Jason Jarvis had his eye on it.

BILBO. It's put me in a bit of a pickle. To be honest.

PEARL. You got your new job at least.

*He looks at his feet.*

Oh fuck off! You're not working for Deliveroo?

BILBO. I can't even ride a bike.

*Beat.* PEARL *looks at him incredulous. Sighs.*

PEARL. Well did you go and see your woman?

BILBO. What, Mina? Went up the offices. But she left six months ago.

PEARL. And she didn't say nothing?

BILBO. What's she gonna say? I spoke to '*Roland*' instead.

PEARL. Was he helpful?

BILBO. He was a fat prick with a lisp. 'The corporate parents' responsibility has ceased, Kevin.' Corporate fucking parent.

PEARL. Kevin?

BILBO. My real name. So I /

PEARL. Why Bill, then?

BILBO. Bilbo – *Lord of the Rings*.

PEARL. Oh yeah. The midget.

BILBO*'s not having this.*

BILBO. He's a *Hobbit*.

PEARL. What *is* a Hobbit?

BILBO. They're like three foot tall. Curly hair. No shoes.

PEARL. You don't look like that.

BILBO. But I love the BOOKS, don't I? Anyway – Roland said. Piss off. Basically.

*Pause.*

PEARL. Ah, Bill. I wish there was…

BILBO. Yeah?

PEARL. Something I could…

    do.                          BILBO. Do?

    Properly. To help.

BILBO. Yeah. Yeah. No / worries.

PEARL. I mean it's not like you could… stay at mine / or anything

BILBO. No.

PEARL. No…

BILBO. No?

PEARL. No. I mean –

BILBO. I get it. I get / it.

PEARL. Mum's on the sofa most nights. I've given up trying to get her upstairs. And Rubes'd do your fucking head in.

BILBO. Ruby's alright.

PEARL. I've just… I got too much on my plate, Bill.

BILBO. Nah nah nah, it's coolio, Pearlie. I'll be alright, won't I? I'm like a dog. I always land on my feet.

PEARL. That's cats.

BILBO. Yeah.

*Beat. She looks at him.*

PEARL. Come here.

BILBO. Why?

PEARL. Just… Come here, you dickhead, I wanna give you a hug.

*He resists but she grabs him and hugs him.*

BILBO. This is weird.

*She hugs him tight. A little of her own sadness might be coming out. She lets him go.*

*Door opens and* FRANK *sticks his head in. They fix themselves up quickly – back to business.*

FRANK. SHOP.

*FRANK comes in, dressed in a beige suit, which is a wee bit worn and withered, and a broad sun hat which has seen better days. He wears sunglasses. He carries a paper. BILBO fixes up in FRANK's presence.*

PEARL. Evening, Mr Parsons.

FRANK. Pearlie: the jewel in our crown!

BILBO. Wotcha, Frank!

FRANK. Alright, trouble.

BILBO. What's that perfume, Pearl?

PEARL. *Beyoncé: Heat.*

BILBO. More like Beyoncé: Feet.

*She whacks him and he kicks her playfully in the arse.*

FRANK. I do like to see the young people enjoying themselves.

PEARL. He's a cheeky bastard, Frank.

FRANK. Language.

PEARL. Soz.

FRANK. Fucking disgraceful.

BILBO. Who you trying to impress?

PEARL. Frank, of course.

FRANK. Oof, if I was thirty years younger.

BILBO. Try fifty.

FRANK. Brains over brawn, Bilbo.

PEARL. BRAWN?

*She squeezes* BILBO*'s non-existent bicep. Tickles him and he whelps near* FRANK*'s ear.*

FRANK (*holding his head*). Not in my ear please.

PEARL. Bit fragile?

FRANK. I feel a bit like I'm in a cloud. Hair of the dog should perk me up.

BILBO. German Shepherd?

FRANK. Very droll.

PEARL. Any nuts?

FRANK. Two thank you, but you're not getting your hands on them.

BILBO. Standard!

PEARL. I'm gonna miss this madness.

FRANK. It's just bants. Isn't it, Bilbo?

BILBO. Just bants, Frank.

PEARL. 'Bants.'

FRANK. No nuts for me... Joanie cooked a stew.

PEARL. Nice?

FRANK. She... struggles with dumplings.

PEARL *goes to pour the Guinness.*

BILBO. No Guinness, Pearl.

PEARL. Oh, shit. No Guinness no John Smiths no Stella no Stout.

BILBO. We're winding it down.

FRANK. What have you got in bottles?

PEARL. Ummmm – (*Looking*.) Carling Zest?

BILBO. Don't touch it. It's evil.

PEARL. Foster's?

FRANK. Fizzy piss? Go on then.

> FRANK *takes a look around the old place*.

> So. It's Really Happening.

PEARL. Yep.

FRANK. No last-chance-saloon, eleventh-hour-miracle?

PEARL. Nope.

FRANK. I was thinking, you know. Surely Lloyd left Kenny quite a bit.

PEARL. So?

FRANK. He must have been sitting on thousands. Not to speak ill of the dead, but Lloyd was a tight bastard.

BILBO. I always forget you knew Ken's dad.

FRANK. We fought like cat and dog but we were muckers.

BILBO. You weren't after Kenny's mum, were you?

FRANK. Don't be a prat! We didn't see eye to eye on politics. I mean, I'm all for trade unions but there is a limit.

PEARL. Lloyd's money went years ago. The nursing home was two grand a week. Dementia's specialist care, isn't it?

FRANK. I had no idea. (*Shivers*.)

PEARL. Anyway it's not a money thing. Now Jarvis is on the scene, Ken don't stand a chance.

FRANK. He's an appalling human.

BILBO. Ken reckons he's a reptilian shape-shifter.

FRANK. Well either way. Jason Jarvis is a C–U–N–T.

PEARL (*mock shock*). FRANK!

BILBO. Ladies present!

FRANK. I won't apologise. It's because of him that... all this is ending.

BILBO/PEARL. Yeah.

*Beat.* FRANK *ponders.*

FRANK. Two *GRAND* a week? A care home? Poor Lloyd.

PEARL. You're alright, you've got Joanie to look after you.

FRANK. Nobody knows what the future holds. (*Takes his hat off and holds it to his chest – turning his face to the sky.*) God strike me down with a smile on my face and a pint in my hand.

PEARL. Well it won't be in here unless he does it tonight.

FRANK. Where is he?

BILBO. Who, God?

FRANK. Kenneth!

PEARL. Upstairs.

FRANK. Okay, is he?

*Beat.* PEARL *glances at* BILBO.

PEARL. Yeah.

FRANK. He'll be king of the road. A great feeling.

FRANK *goes to his seat but he stops and turns to them – to sing the third, fourth and fifth line of 'King of the Road' by Roger Miller.* PEARL *and* BILBO *stop to listen to him, humour him.*

FRANK *does a little bowing gesture at the end. They might give him a little clap.*

PEARL. How long did it take you to do The Knowledge?

FRANK. Three years.

BILBO. Oh my GOD.

FRANK. That's quicker than most. I just wanted to beat Lloyd.

BILBO. And did you?

FRANK. By six months! He was a sore loser.

    PEARL *and* BILBO *go about their business.* FRANK *sits down and opens his paper.*

PEARL. Pressure's low on this.

BILBO. It's running out.

PEARL/BILBO. When it's gone it's gone.

PEARL. Jinx.

    *They link pinky fingers. Beat.*

BILBO. How many streets?

FRANK. Twenty-five thousand.

PEARL. Wow.

BILBO. I can't even remember my pin.

FRANK. All in the hippocampus. The wealth of information actually makes the brain bigger.

BILBO. Yeah?

FRANK. This hat is an extra-large.

    *Beat.*

    Kenny'll have to watch it.

    FRANK *mimes drinking. Then, conspiratorially:*

    Affects the cognitive functioning!

BILBO (*slightly defensive*). At least he's off the firewater.

    PEARL*'s phone starts to ring again. She is frustrated.*

PEARL. Ruby, I'm at work!

FRANK. Just because he drinks Foster's from a half-glass. But he doesn't fool me. I've seen him put away more than twenty in a day.

PEARL. Well stop her!

*PEARL covers the mouthpiece.*

Mum's moving furniture again.

*She hurries out.*

BILBO. He's alright.

FRANK. It's funny, you know. When I was a young man I moved *into* London to do The Knowledge. Now Kenny starts doing it and he's moving *out*.

BILBO. Don't seem right.

FRANK. What?

BILBO. A London. Without Kenny.

FRANK (*raises his glass*). Change.

*He drinks.*

How's he doing with the runs?

*BILBO looks at him, confused.*

BILBO. Oh you mean the taxi runs! I was testing him yesterday. He got stuck on a right nightmare. That vein popped out of his head.

FRANK (*pointing to his temple*). This one here?

BILBO. Yeah.

*Beat. FRANK is sheepish.*

FRANK. I wanted to say… thank you, Bilbo.

BILBO. What? Oh for the other… day, nah no / worries.

FRANK. I didn't say it properly at the time.

BILBO. Well you were a bit…

FRANK. I wasn't pissed!

BILBO. I know. It was seven in the morning!

FRANK. I hadn't slept well the night before and… It was just a dizzy slip. Right on the arse though. You didn't tell anyone, did you?

BILBO. Course not. I'm just glad I found ya! You should have let me take you home, though. See you in and all that.

FRANK. Joanie patched me up.

*Beat.*

BILBO. Never seen inside one of them maisonettes, as it goes. Just a one-bed, is it?

FRANK (*unsure*). Two.

BILBO. You just have that as a spare room then, do you?

FRANK. It's… where Bridgette stays. When she visits.

BILBO. Oh… right.

*He polishes the glass.*

It's only that. I've got a bit of a gap.

FRANK. A gap?

BILBO. Between places.

*Unbearable pause.* FRANK *begins to laugh nervously.*

FRANK. No. Don't think so.

BILBO. You'd hardly know I was there, Frank /

FRANK. Joanie wouldn't like it.

BILBO (*hurt*). I wouldn't nick nothing.

FRANK. Of course. I didn't think… Look. We're too old for houseguests. Old farts that we are. Sorry, old man.

BILBO *sighs. Nods.*

BILBO. 'S alright. I'm going for a fag. Tell Kenny I've gone for a shit.

FRANK. Over and out. Bilbo – what was the nightmare?

BILBO. The what?

FRANK. The run. That Kenneth got stuck on.

BILBO. Oh. Vauxhall Bridge Road to Cold Harbour Lane.

BILBO *disappears*. FRANK *finds this quite funny. Like it's an easy run.*

FRANK. Vauxhall Bridge Road to Cold Harbour Lane??
Forward onto
Forward onto
Gardens! Something with a P? Or a B? Or a D?
You see it swims a bit
Sort of melts into
(*Closes his eyes – focuses hard.*)
BESSBOROUGH!
Bullseye!
There she is! Forward onto Bessborough Gardens and onto
(*Suddenly distracted by another memory.*)
Steps
Steps of a
Somewhere
Saint somewhere
Saint with a J
James or a John or a
Steeples! And bunting
and kisses in the rain and
Joanie and lace and confetti in her hair and

*Beat. He steers himself back.*

Forward onto Vauxhall Bridge
Forward onto
Slip into
Forward onto
Into
What is it?
What is it?
With the spies

The name's Bond
MI5!
Or it is 6
or is it

*Beat.*

Chickens! And sheep and goats
And why am I
Why do I
What do you call it a...
City Farm!
Bridgette likes the goats best
Likes their funny faces
Goofy teeth
Handfuls of feed and pink lips and giggling girls and
Me and my two giggling girls
Forward onto the big lane
Joanie with her coal-black hair and her pale face and tiny
little ankles and wrists.
Red lips...

*He gets lost in the memory for a moment*

Just stick to the present.
'The past is a foreign country' as they say.
Could get lost there, very easily...

PEARL *enters, angry, walks to the bar.* FRANK *fixes up.*

PEARL. Fucking ridiculous.

FRANK. What is?

*The phone rings again.* PEARL *answers it.*

PEARL. NO.

*She hangs up, throws it down on the bar.* PEARL *rests her head on her arms, on the bar.*

FRANK. Mum?

PEARL *groans in affirmation.*

Real bad, is she?

PEARL. Tonight of all nights, Mum!

PEARL *looks so forlorn.*

FRANK (*conspiratorially*). Want a little drink?

PEARL. Nah. Just makes it worse.

FRANK. Wise. You know, Joanie got a bit... blue after Bridgette was born. Do you know how she beat it?

PEARL (*she gets this a lot*). Frank, I'm not being funny but... /

FRANK. She swam, Pearl. She swam and swam and swam. And Mum could do with the exercise.

PEARL (*defensive*). That's the meds. They bloat her out.

FRANK. A swim might cheer her up.

PEARL (*exasperated*). She's on a high right now! She doesn't *need* cheering up. She needs fucking tasering!

FRANK. Steady.

PEARL. I'll get in tonight, and I'll fall arse over tit in the dark because she's rearranged the furniture again!

FRANK *smiles at her.*

Piss off. It's not funny.

FRANK *chuckles.* PEARL *laughs too eventually. It fades.*

Sometimes I hate her.

FRANK. Don't hate. Don't do that, Pearlie.

PEARL. I know she's ill but... Sometimes I want to smash her in the face with my fist. Sorry.

*Beat.*

FRANK. Thought we might see her in here last night. For old times' sake.

PEARL. You probably wouldn't recognise her.

FRANK. Poor Fiona. She used to light up this place.

PEARL *looks at him. She is always interested in hearing about her mum when she was younger.*

The boys used to say she looked like Madonna.

PEARL. Now she looks like Maradona.

*They laugh a bit. It fades.*

FRANK. Sad. She just had a spark.

*Beat.* PEARL *might go back to what she's doing for a moment.*

PEARL. Am I like her?

FRANK *looks up.*

Like she was then?

FRANK. No.

PEARL. No?

FRANK. No.

PEARL. Oh.

*Beat.*

FRANK. You've got a good strong head on your shoulders. (*Beat.*) I suppose it'll be easier after tonight. To keep her in check.

PEARL *shudders internally, deep resentment wells up.*

PEARL. Yeah.

FRANK. Keep her away from those – what do you call them?

PEARL. Players.

FRANK. They've always been Fi's problem. Always thought she would ride away into the sunset with them. Behind great pain, there's always a man.

PEARL. Is that a quote? Did someone actually say that?

FRANK. I think I did.

PEARL. Well it's bollocks.

FRANK. I beg your / pardon.

PEARL. She had us, weren't we enough?

FRANK. You're young, Pearlie! You don't understand. When you get down to the real slog of life, it's lonely on your own. I know I have a moan about Joanie, a little joke but… I couldn't be without her.

*Beat. A change of direction.* PEARL *is genuinely curious.*

PEARL. Frank, I'm not being funny but – you're *always* in here. You must hardly see each other.

FRANK. We have our rhythms. Have you ever known me to leave here after eleven? I get back to do her Ovaltine every night and I *must* be compis mentis. She won't abide instant!

PEARL. OH MY GOD, FRANK, that's so cute!

FRANK. I've never been cute in my life!

PEARL. Seriously, you and Joanie are 'relationship goals'.

FRANK. Are we indeed?

PEARL. When you got married it *meant* something. Till death do us part. (*Beat.*) I love old things.

FRANK. Oh ta very much!

PEARL. Nah – I mean – like I loved doing stuff like World War II at school. 'Blitz spirit'… is it?

FRANK. Oh yes.

PEARL. And people would wear a pair of shoes for *years*.

FRANK. Make do and mend. We didn't have your Primark!

PEARL. People *valued* things.

FRANK. Maybe you were born in the wrong era.

PEARL. Maybe.

*Beat.* FRANK *considers whether to ask:*

FRANK. No special chap in your life then?

PEARL. Nah.

FRANK. Or a special… lass?

PEARL *laughs*.

This is 2016 you know, Pearlie!

PEARL. No special lass, Frank.

FRANK. A boy then.

PEARL. I never said that!

FRANK. No. But you lit up a bit.

SHAUN *enters. Wearing jeans and a T-shirt – possibly a vest, freshly showered from work. He has a big bag with him.*

SHAUN. What's the craic, lads?

FRANK. Pearl was just telling me about her love life.

SHAUN. You sure the aul ticker can take it, Frank?

PEARL. My love life would *bore* you to death.

SHAUN. Never. Give us a pint of Stella there.

PEARL. Stella's off. *Foster's*?

SHAUN. No don't give me any of that shite. What's them bottles there?

PEARL. Carling Zest. It's cheap. BOGOF.

SHAUN. Sure, I've only just walked in the door.

PEARL. Buy One Get One Free, you clown!

SHAUN. Aye go on. Put me down for two. I'll hold me nose.

*He flashes her a smile. He likes making her laugh.*

FRANK (*without looking up from his paper*). Lie back and think of England.

SHAUN *chuckles. Takes a swig.*

SHAUN. Mmm. Not bad that. Fruity.

SHAUN *sits at the bar.*

Glad he decided to open tonight. My roommate's trimming his pubes.

PEARL. What, Raf? YUCK /

FRANK. Ugh. Why?

SHAUN. Calls it 'manscaping'. Says the girls like it. Hey, Pearlie /

PEARL. Don't ask me!

FRANK *does a big old yawn.*

SHAUN. Keeping you up, Frankie-boy?

PEARL (*to* SHAUN). Didn't see you leave last night?

SHAUN. Sloped off about two. I was steaming, man.

PEARL. You didn't seem it.

SHAUN. No? I was shaking like a shitting dog this morning.

BILBO *comes back.*

Here he is! The Lord of the Ring.

BILBO. Carling Zest? Do you want an umbrella with that, Shaun?

SHAUN. Aye, and a pineapple chunk too, Dildo! Where's the man then?

PEARL. Bill, have a look.

BILBO *disappears up the stairs. Beat.*

SHAUN. How's Joanie?

FRANK (*not looking up*). She's alright, if you like that sort of thing.

BILBO *enters.*

BILBO. The shower's going and he's playing The Specials at top volume.

PEARL. I'm not sure if that's a good or bad thing.

SHAUN (*spots something on the bottle*). Jesus Christ! These went out of date in 2014.

PEARL. Shit, do you wanna change it?

SHAUN. You're alright, love. I've started so I'll finish.

FRANK (*not looking up*). Said the actress to the bishop.

*They both drink. He continues looking at the label.*

SHAUN. THIS IS FUCKING TWO-POINT-EIGHT PER CENT!

FRANK. Two-point-eight?          PEARL. It's not!

BILBO. HA!

SHAUN *wipes his mouth*

SHAUN. I can't drink that, Pearlie. That's fucking. Sacrilege that is. Change it for a pint of fizzy piss.

PEARL. Yeah course.

*She pours a pint of Foster's. SHAUN looks at his phone. A lull.*

FRANK. I say. A friend of mine's just revealed that he's become a world-famous mime artist.

SHAUN (*not looking up*). Oh yeah?

FRANK. Yeah. I said 'You kept that one quiet.'

PEARL. Did you listen to the playlist?

FRANK (*shaking his head*). Philistines.

SHAUN. I can't work fuck-all out on this phone, love.

PEARL. It's called *Divas*. It's got Beyoncé, Alicia Keys, bit of Amy.

SHAUN. Sounds great – I just can' t / get it to

PEARL. Pass it. I'll have a look.

*He hesitates for a moment, then passes his phone and takes the pint.*

SHAUN. Don't be looking at the pictures mind.

BILBO. As if you've got dick pics.

SHAUN. Who said anything about dicks?

*She takes his phone.*

Wild impressed our Luke was. When I said I had 'Spotify' on me phone.

PEARL *smiles.*

BILBO. Did you tell him you don't know how to open it?

SHAUN. Get te fuck, Dildo.

PEARL. I'm putting that Chaka Khan one on there too.

SHAUN. 'Ain't Nobody'. Best song of the eighties.

FRANK. What's all this?

SHAUN. Me and Pearl are swapping music. I'm giving her a bit of Sade, a bit of Randy...

*This reminds* BILBO.

BILBO. Oh yeah. Tunes.

*He ducks down behind the bar.*

FRANK. And what's she giving you in return?

PEARL. What?                    SHAUN. Ya what?

BILBO (*from below*). Has anyone seen the connector?

FRANK. Some caterwauling teenybopper I suppose?

PEARL. Er... excuse me?

SHAUN. Some of it's not bad, you know, Frank. I like a bit of that Beyoncé.

BILBO (*laughing*). I bet you do, mate.

SHAUN. Her *music*, Dildo. And Florence Against the Machine.

PEARL. Florence *and* the Machine. /

SHAUN. And the Winehouse of course. She's the real deal.

FRANK. A tragic soul.

PEARL (*to* SHAUN). Come here then.

*She's got her earphones out of her phone and attached them to his phone. They have one earphone each.*

SHAUN. You smell nice, what's that?

PEARL. Dunno.

SHAUN. You dunno?

PEARL. It's just me.

BILBO *pops up from behind the bar with a clipboard.*

BILBO. Have you lot got a death wish or what?

SHAUN. What?

BILBO. He'll go apeshit if he finds this.

SHAUN. Pass it here.

BILBO *passes the clipboard.*

FRANK. Where do we stand, Mr Walker?

SHAUN *checks the stairs and bar entrance.*

SHAUN. Fourteen on luxury flats. Two for reopening as a traditional boozer.

BILBO. Fat chance.

SHAUN. Six on 'Wankers' pub'.

FRANK. How do you qualify that? /

BILBO. It'll be luxury flats.

SHAUN. Eight on restaurant. Two on 'Gastric pub'.

BILBO. Flats. /

FRANK. 'Gastric'?

PEARL. Eileen.

FRANK. Bless her.

BILBO. Jarvis'll get nine flats on this site.

SHAUN. Jesus, does that say 'mosque'?

PEARL. It says 'Morris'! You need glasses.

*They both find this very funny.*

SHAUN. No, Morris needs to sort his handwriting, man!

FRANK. One more punt.

SHAUN. What you after?

FRANK. Another two quid on flats.

BILBO. You lot!

SHAUN. Just a bit of fun, Dildo. Pearlie?

PEARL. Nah.

BILBO. Pearl knows.

PEARL. I'm skint.

SHAUN. I'll cover you, what you after?

PEARL. You got Tesco Express down there?

BILBO. PEARL! /

SHAUN. *Tesco Express…* Like your style!

KENNY. Good evening good evening!

KENNY *enters – they quickly hide the clipboard –* PEARL
*whisking it behind her back.* KENNY*'s cut himself shaving.
He's wearing an incredibly loud shirt. He carries a durable*

*supermarket bag for life. He pops the bag on the bar. Taps it gently as though settling it down. Throughout, he glances frequently to the pub entrance and checks his phone.*

SHAUN. Kenny lad!          PEARL. Here he is!

KENNY. Mr Walker!

FRANK. Could somebody pass my sunglasses?

KENNY. Nobody panic, I'm down, I am here!

BILBO. You alright?          PEARL. You've cut yourself
                                               shaving.

KENNY. Don't fuss.

*He points to* PEARL, *gestures behind her back.*

Goodbye card?

PEARL. Don't spoil it.

KENNY. You lot are too good to me.

*He bangs the bar three times.*

DRINK!

*He grabs himself a half-glass – goes straight to the Foster's tap – stops. He thinks 'Fuck it' and swaps it for a pint glass, spins it in his hand and pours a pint.*

SHAUN. Well no one told us it was a fancy-dress?

KENNY. This, Mr Walker, is my lucky shirt.

FRANK. Yes it looks a bit like a bird's shat on it.

KENNY. Cost me forty quid. In *1998*! Rocha John Rocha, mate. No fucking about.

PEARL. What's in the bag?

KENNY. Nothing. Just some bits.

*He takes a big sip of his pint. Swooshes it in his cheeks as though he was tasting wine.*

Mmm… A medium malty character with a fruity aroma and the merest suggestion of – (*Takes a big sniff.*) chicken tikka masala. BOOM!

*He laughs. They all laugh. For a moment, it's all good.*

Bill, you have that – I've only had a bit out of it –

BILBO. Oh nice one.

KENNY. Pearl – (*Sings the girly drinks, grabbing and spinning her around.*) Babycham? Malibu?

PEARL (*pulling away, laughing*). Piss off! I'm not drinking and if I was I'd have a BEER. Thanks.

KENNY. Come on, you lot! Lively yourselves up. Frank! A Guinness, sir?

FRANK. Can't.

KENNY. On the house.

FRANK. Guinness is finished.

KENNY. What, seriously?

SHAUN. Stella too. This one's had me drinking Carling *Zest*.

KENNY. Jesus.

PEARL. That's all that's left. When it's gone it's gone, you said. Why are you limping?

KENNY. I've got a wet sock, haven't I? Some dilbert left a mug of coffee outside my door.

*He glances at* BILBO.

BILBO. Sorry.

KENNY. Let's have a little livener. What have we got? (*Lifts the vodka, then the gin, humming to himself, lifts a few more bottles – there's not much left in any of them. He's bereft for a moment. Then:*) Hang on. I've got a plan, Stan.

*He moves towards the cellar.*

BILBO. I'll go.

KENNY. No, only I know what I'm looking for.

*He disappears then pops his head back round for* BILBO.

'There is only one Lord of the Ring, only one who can bend it to his will.'

KENNY/BILBO (*joining in quote*). 'And he does not share power!'

SHAUN. No one's bending my ring.

KENNY. You get some tunes on, Bill.

BILBO. Yeah yeah. What?

KENNY (*calling back*). Anything you like, as long as it's not Bruno fucking Mars.

*He disappears. They look at each other.*

SHAUN. Seems to be holding it together.

BILBO *ducks down under the counter. Blur's 'London Loves' comes on.*

FRANK. What's in the bag for life?

SHAUN *has a little poke at the bag.*

SHAUN. More than a bag for life, that. Strong. A bag for the afterlife too.

FRANK. An infinity bag.

SHAUN. 'An infinity bag.' I like that, Frank.

BILBO *pops back up.*

BILBO. Ken won't like it.

SHAUN. Oh chill out, Dildo. Here, is this a –

KENNY *reappears holding a crate.*

KENNY. CAMPARI!

*He slams the crate down.*

PEARL. Oh God.            SHAUN. Jesus.

Nobody drinks that except Pissy Richard.

KENNY. There's crates of this downstairs.

KENNY *goes about getting glasses.*

FRANK. He was gazebo'd last / night.

SHAUN. Absolutely mortal.

KENNY. He'd had a bit of bad news.

PEARL. Oh, what?

KENNY. Can't tell you that can I? The Pub Landlord is the Keeper of Secrets. The proletarian's therapist. The laymen's confidant.

SHAUN (*to* PEARL). Probably got crabs.

PEARL *laughs at this.*

PEARL. He should try some manscaping.

SHAUN *laughs at this.*

FRANK. He stole my hat at one point. Pearl had to kick him.

SHAUN. Girl power, eh?

PEARL. Yellow belt in Taekwondo, mate.

FRANK (*takes hat off and looks in it*). Still a bit greasy.

KENNY *goes about pouring shots.*

SHAUN. I had a lost night on the Campari once. In the early nineties. All I remember is that I had a mullet and I lost a shoe.

KENNY. 'A Campari, a Mullet, a Missing Shoe.' It's like poetry, Mr Walker.

PEARL. Can't imagine you with a mullet.

SHAUN. Trendsetter me, love. I was the first person on our estate to get a shell suit. And the first to realise they were shite.

PEARL. They're coming back in.

SHAUN. Well they can fuck right off out again! My mate caught the sleeve of his on a lighter flame – turned him into a human fireball.

PEARL *really laughs at this.*

KENNY. Shaun.

*He passes the drink.* SHAUN *holds it aloft. Shudders.*

SHAUN. I can confirm, people, that this tastes exactly the same coming up as it does going down.

PEARL. Nice.

SHAUN *goes to sip it.*

KENNY. No no, Mr Walker, let's have some decorum. Bill.

KENNY *passes him a shot of the thick red liquid.* BILBO *is surprised when he gets one.*

BILBO. Wow.

KENNY. And Pearlie!

PEARL. Nah I'm alright /

KENNY (*a little too sharply*). No no come on. No excuses!

*He makes her take one.*

Frankie-boy?

FRANK. I'll take whatever's going.

FRANK *takes it. They hold the drinks up.* KENNY*'s got a sheen of sweat on his brow.*

KENNY. Okay. (*Laughs a bit. Glances to door.*) To… endings. To… beginnings. To The Anchor.

ALL. The Anchor.

*They drink. Beat.*

KENNY. Fuck.                         SHAUN. Shite, man.

FRANK. Language.

KENNY. And – and – to the best bar staff this side of the river.

*He grabs* BILBO *and* PEARL *both behind the neck.*

What am I gonna do without my gruesome twosome?
Without Pearlie the Kung Fu Panda? Without Bill dropping
such deadly guffs in the cellar that the ale turns to vinegar.

BILBO. You can talk! Yours smell like baby poo.

*They laugh.*

KENNY. Nah. My loss is Deliveroo's gain, mate.

BILBO *and* PEARL *share a look.*

PEARL. Actually Bill ain't doing that now.

BILBO. Pearl.

KENNY. No?

SHAUN. Why? Can you not ride a bike?

FRANK *and* SHAUN *laugh.*

BILBO. Nah but they treat you like shite, don't they?

KENNY *is distracted. Looking at the door.*

KENNY. Do they?

BILBO. Yeah.

KENNY (*with a cloth*). Gonna… wipe down. Outside.

KENNY *exits.* FRANK *goes back to his paper.*

BILBO. How's work, Shaun?

SHAUN. Work is work, Bilbo.

BILBO. Right.

*Beat.*

FRANK. It's Chinese Year of the Monkey.

BILBO. Busy? Is it?

SHAUN. Building a thousand flats, a whole new retail village and an extension to the Northern Line? Yeah, fairly busy, mate.

BILBO. I just wondered if there was any work going.

KENNY *comes back in, overhearing the last bit.*

KENNY. You'd do worse, Mr Walker. What he lacks in skill he makes up for in enthusiasm.

SHAUN. What sort a work?

BILBO. Whatever it is you do.

KENNY. Specificity, Bilbo.

SHAUN. I'm a scaffolder. I been doing this thirty years, lad.

BILBO. I was thinking I could… learn on the job.

PEARL. Bill, aren't you scared of heights?

FRANK *and* SHAUN *laugh.* BILBO *looks at* PEARL. PEARL *mouths 'sorry'.*

BILBO. Just forget it, yeah?

KENNY. Oh, Mr Baggins.

SHAUN. A scaffolder with vertigo! You crack me up, Dildo!

PEARL. Look. Bill's had a bit of a mare. Innit, Bill?

BILBO. Don't matter.

FRANK. There's no job at Battersea Power Station for the likes of you, Bilbo.

BILBO. What, you mean stupid?

FRANK. No I mean British.

PEARL. Oh not this again.        KENNY. Spare us, Frankie.

FRANK. How many Brits are there, Shaun, would you say?

SHAUN. Can't speak for the whole site, but on our team? It's about eighty per cent from Europe. Outside Britain, like.

FRANK. Exactly.

KENNY *plops a carboard box with the word 'BREXIT' scrawled on it and a slit in the top in front of* FRANK.

KENNY. That's one pound please.

FRANK. But I never even said the B-word!

SHAUN. Aye but you were          KENNY. Yeah but you were
    thinking it.                          thinking it.

FRANK. Who are you two, the thought police?

PEARL. Can we focus on a way to help Bill please?

BILBO. Nah forget it, / Pearl.

FRANK. Trigger the Thingy. Take control. That *would* help
    Bill. They'll be a job for him then.

KENNY. That's defo fifty pee.

FRANK. For 'Thingy'?

KENNY. You meant Article 50. It's a quid for the B-word itself
    and fifty pee for relating terminology.

FRANK (*rummaging in his pocket*). Rules and regs – this is *like*
    the bloody EU!

    SHAUN *and* PEARL *look at each other, eyes roll. They
    think it's faded and they can move on – and then –*

    British jobs for the British working classes! Property built
    *for* us, *by* us.

KENNY. But they're not *for us* are they? Not unless you got
    a spare million lying around.

SHAUN. Two.

KENNY. Silly me. Two million.

SHAUN. Most of the first phase sold to overseas fellas anyway.

KENNY. Who'll keep 'em empty.

FRANK. Breaks my heart.

*Beat. They drink.*

PEARL (*to* SHAUN). Does it bother you?

*He sighs a little, looks at* PEARL.

SHAUN. I just build them.

PEARL. Oh yeah. I didn't / mean like

SHAUN. I work hard. Have a laugh. Get paid. Have a few pints with yous in the week and then jump on the train back to The Pool for the weekend.

PEARL. Yeah.

SHAUN. You know me and politics, Pearlie.

FRANK. I'm going back to my paper now.

BILBO. I might put my name down for a rooftop penthouse.

SHAUN. You'd be lucky to get in the bin cupboard.

PEAR (*quietly*). Shaun.

SHAUN. What?

PEARL *shakes the box.*

PEARL. Quite a lot in here. Right, Bill. When we're done – you're getting this. Put towards a deposit. Or keep you in rollies.

BILBO. Ken said it's for a charity of his choice.

PEARL. Ken, what's the charity of your choice?

KENNY. I was gonna give it to donkeys.

PEARL. Can you give it to Bilbo?

KENNY. Yeah. Same diff.

BILBO. Nah, I couldn't…

PEARL. Charity begins at home, mate. It's yours.

SHAUN (*shaking another box*). Here, there's quite a bit in the Trump box too. Ah shite. I don't have to pay for that, do I?

KENNY. I'll let you off.

FRANK. I'm looking forward to November. Then we'll never have to talk about him again!

KENNY. Never say never, Frankie.

FRANK. Getting out of Europe is about taking back control. It makes *sense*. But that orange buffoon? With his little hands and his big ego? And no doubt his microscopic penis?

SHAUN *and* PEARL *enjoy a giggle about this.*

DONALD TRUMP? People aren't morons.

PEARL. That's /

FRANK. Yes I know and I don't mind because it's for Bilbo.

FRANK *rummages again.*

BILBO. Cheers, Frank.

FRANK *puts a fiver in the box.*

FRANK. No problem.

KENNY (*raises glass*). A toast: To the end of the world as we know it.

BILBO *addresses the audience.*

BILBO. And tonight rolls on. Like any night.

Me and Kenny and Pearl – we're tight – got our rhythms behind this bar. Like a sort of slick machine. Them two in charge, I'm happy just to be a cog. 'Cept tonight, Kenny's odd. Sort of out of step. With us. Keeps checking his watch, looking over to the door. What's he waiting for? 'Where are they all?'

Eating wankerburgers at The Hand and Flower? Burritos at The Ship? Craft ale at The Union?

Is it pulled pork, vegan or gluten-free eats, or giant jenga or super-speedy broadband.

Which Kenny won't get. Cos 'A PUB'S FOR TALKING AND FOR GETTING WET'.

The Anchor's like him. It does what it says on the tin.

Or are they at home? With a can. Right-swiping some next girl or man.

Tonight's the usual crowd. Slow and steady. Eileen and Eddie, like every night in the week. The weekend's for daytrips to Margate or Deal; sand between their toes and chips in salty air. But here they just sit and stare. Never say a fucking word. Is that love?

There's Rampant Raf – Shaun's roommate. With his freshly trimmed pubes and his winning smile. Just popping out for a while – see what 'peach-ka' Pimlico has in store. Then four fat Yanks from the hotel near the Tube. In search of 'local beer' and 'authentic British food'. (Well. Foster's is local Ken says. In Melbourne.) Course they're out of luck but stay for a gin as the pub is so 'quaint' like an 'old English Inn'.

I watch drinks downed, mouths wiped, hands shaken, goodbyes said.
And the fact that this is all ending
It just
does my fucking head.
You know?
Like
All of the people
All of the words
Where do they
go?

And when Shaun's in the shitter and Pearl's popped home
I know like I shouldn't leave Ken alone
But I don't know how to
I just have to

*He exits.*

KENNY (*from off*). FUCKING FOUND IT.

> KENNY *pops up from behind the bar with a giant foam pointing finger or other amusing object.*

Bill, are you –

> *He looks around.*

Skiving fuck.

> *He drops the object.* FRANK *is snoozing in the corner. He glances at the bag, pats the top of it. Looks to the door.*

> *The sound of a toilet flushing and* SHAUN *re-enters.*

SHAUN. I'd give it a while.

> *Beat.*

Try six months. Ken?

KENNY. Yeah?

SHAUN. I'm saying I destroyed your toilet, man.

KENNY. What, literally?

SHAUN. Nah... Metaphorically.

KENNY. Don't spose it matters now. Go and give it a kicking!

SHAUN. I don't really wanna go back in there to be honest.

> *They laugh a bit.*

You alright?

KENNY. Pukka.

SHAUN. I'm sorry about tomorrow, mate.

> KENNY *shifts uncomfortably.*

KENNY. 'S okay.

SHAUN. I could come after six?

KENNY (*confused*). After six to... oh to move the stuff!

SHAUN. I can borrow the van then and all.

KENNY. Ah forget it. I can get it all in the back of the Pinto.

SHAUN. What, *everything*?

KENNY. I've sold a bit. I'm leaving a lot – let Jarvis sort it.

SHAUN. Some good stuff up there.

KENNY. I wanna throw off the trappings, mate. Start afresh.

SHAUN. Good man.

KENNY. Anyway it's furnished, the new place, so…

SHAUN. What are the other peeps like?

KENNY. Oh you know. Other young professionals, like myself.

SHAUN. Ha.

KENNY. I'll hardly be there. I mean *you* share a *dorm* with other lads, don't ya? I only have to share a kitchen and a pisser with 'em.

SHAUN (*slightly indignant*). I get to go home at the weekends, like.

KENNY. Oh course. I'll be out doing my runs most of the time.

SHAUN. You'll be coining it in when you've got your cab going. Come back to Pimlico in a blaze of glory – get yourself one of them Nine Elms flats. Fuck the brewery. Fuck Jarvis.

KENNY. I'll drink to that.

*Beat. They drink.*

SHAUN. What's Chatham like?

KENNY. Well…

SHAUN. They say Kent's 'the garden of England'.

KENNY (*unsure*). Yeah. (*Beat.*) It's just a base. Tell you what I'm gonna do, mate, once I get there.

SHAUN. Go on.

KENNY. Sleep in. I *love* sleeping in.

SHAUN. Oh yeah. Wake up with Phil and Holly.

KENNY. Willabooby.

SHAUN. Yep.

KENNY. Mind you, knowing my luck it'll be Ruth and fucking Eamonn.

SHAUN. Ha. Aye.

*Beat. Drink.*

I'll try and keep an eye out. For Bilbo, like.

KENNY. Oh yeah, nice one.

SHAUN. He's gonna struggle without yez.

KENNY. He's nearly twenty-four.

SHAUN. Aye, but he's not like the rest of us.

*Beat.* SHAUN *spies something in the bag for life.*

Is there something you're not telling me, Kenneth?

KENNY. You what?

SHAUN *holds up a classy midi-length flowery dress.*

SHAUN. You're not going all gender fluid on us, are ya?

KENNY *grabs the dress.*

KENNY. Get your mucky paws off it, you savage.

SHAUN. Alright! Alright!

KENNY. It's Orla's.

SHAUN. Oh. Sorry, mate.

KENNY. She's popping in tonight – pick up the last of her stuff.

SHAUN. Oh. That's...

KENNY. Yeah.

*Beat*. KENNY *smooths the dress*.

SHAUN. It's a nice dress.

KENNY *relaxes a bit*.

KENNY. I bought her this. Cath Kidston. I mean, she changed the size. I thought she looked like an eight. But she was a twelve.

SHAUN. I bet she loved you for that!

KENNY. I don't understand women's clothes.

SHAUN. Me neither.

*Beat*.

Never met your Orla.

KENNY. Fucking gorgeous she is. She could be a model. Catalogues.

SHAUN. Tasty.

KENNY. I used to say she had an English Rose complexion. To piss her off. Cos she was Irish.

SHAUN. Haha. How long's it been?

KENNY. Too long, mate. Do I… I look… alright? Just…

SHAUN. Yeah yeah yeah. Although you know you've got a massive booger?

KENNY. Have I?

SHAUN. I'm joking, you thick cunt.

KENNY. Oh nice. Fuck you very much.

SHAUN. You're fine.

*They laugh*.

KENNY. She couldn't believe it. About this place going. Me moving to Kent. All that.

SHAUN. Lotta changes, mate. Lotta changes.

*KENNY nods. They drink.*

KENNY. I hope.

SHAUN. What?

KENNY. I hope I... make it.

*Beat.*

SHAUN. What do you mean, man?

KENNY. I just hope I can – I hope I can make it.

*Unchartered territory for SHAUN.*

SHAUN. You know what, mate? One day you'll wake up in the morning and you'll just be like – oh another day. You know.

KENNY. Yeah yeah yeah. (*Beat.*) No whaddya mean?

SHAUN. I mean these things. These... tough times, they pass. And you get it back. You get it back.

KENNY. Get what back?

*Pause.*

SHAUN. Hope.

*Beat.*

KENNY. Yeah. Oh yeah yeah yeah yeah yeah. Bags of it, mate. Gotta have. In this world.

*PEARL rushes in.*

PEARL. Sorry sorry sorry sorry sorry sorry sorry sorry –

KENNY. What am I paying you minimum wage for???

PEARL. Sorry sorry, Ken.

*PEARL gets behind the bar. Starts wiping down.*

KENNY. What's up with Fi?

PEARL. Nothing.

KENNY. Come on. Where is it this week?

SHAUN. Eh?

KENNY. Fi gets 'the wanderlust bug'.

SHAUN. Oh right yeah.

PEARL *stops wiping*.

PEARL. Devon. Sea air for Ruby. Garden for her. She wants to live in a fisherman's cottage! It's these bloody property programmes! She's got hundreds of them saved on the planner. She'd actually started packing, Ken!

KENNY. Bloody hell.

SHAUN. A change might be good for her, Pearlie. Good for you all.

PEARL (*snaps*). We can't afford 'change'! We've been in that flat twenty years!

KENNY (*gently*). Alright alright.

PEARL. Sorry, Shaun. It's just.

SHAUN. You're alright, love. /

PEARL. It's just all around us people have bought them up and sold them on for stupid money. Esther and Basil's old flat sold for half a mil last month.

KENNY. Old-fashioned notion, mate. Social housing. Five years' time – it won't exist. It'll be Hunger Games and shitting in the gutter.

PEARL. It's only Mum and Mrs Bosu that's still council on our floor. And if she hands in our notice? What then?

KENNY *gets up from where he's sitting*.

KENNY. Pearlie, sit down.

PEARL. I don't wanna sit down.

KENNY. Have a drink then.

PEARL. I don't wanna drink.

*Beat. She grabs a glass.*

Fuck it I'll have a drink.

SHAUN. Good girl, yourself.

*KENNY clasps PEARL's hand as she goes to pour herself a pint.*

KENNY. No seriously, Pearlie, have a drink on me.

*He hands her a little wodge of notes. SHAUN isn't really watching.*

PEARL. Oh – Ken I can't /

*KENNY puts his finger to his lips. PEARL goes about getting herself a drink.*

KENNY. What a shite state of affairs.

SHAUN/PEARL. Yeah...

KENNY. Everything feels like it's falling apart.

SHAUN/PEARL. Yeah...

*KENNY goes to the door, looks out.*

PEARL (*quietly*). Sorry, about before.

SHAUN. Couldn't matter less, gorgeous. /

KENNY (*looks back at the empty pub*). Look at this place. Like the *Mary Celeste*. I know we get the tourists. And your lot – contractors and that. But this is a locals' pub, innit, really. And what's the problem with locals?

SHAUN. Go on.

KENNY. They die.

SHAUN. Inconsiderate bastards.

KENNY. Frank's halfway there already!

FRANK (*without moving*). I'm not dead I'm conserving energy!

*He makes them all jump. And then laugh.*

PEARL. God you made me / jump!

SHAUN. You were snoring earlier, Frank!

*FRANK checks his watch.*

FRANK. Well, must wake up. It's time for bed.

*He makes a few moves to get his stuff together but then closes his eyes again.*

KENNY (*to* PEARL). You wouldn't come in here if you didn't work here – would ya?

PEARL (*joking*). Hell no!

SHAUN. Ah Pearl would be sipping cocktails at The Clarendon wouldn't ye?

PEARL. If I didn't work here I'd be at home right now doing Ruby's science homework.

SHAUN. Bill would come in though.

KENNY/PEARL. Yeah.

SHAUN. You'll never get rid of Bilbo!

PEARL. Here, did you know his real name's Kevin?

SHAUN. Kevin?

PEARL. I don't think he looks like a Kevin.

SHAUN. You look like a Pearl.

PEARL. What all hard and round and little?

KENNY (*not listening*). Nope: the arse has fallen out of the pub game. It's fucking finished.

*KENNY looks anguished for a moment.*

SHAUN. You've had a good innings, mate.

KENNY. I'm not dying.

SHAUN. No, what I mean is –

PEARL. He means you've had some good times, Ken. Some great nights.

KENNY. Yeah.

KENNY *reminisces for a moment, wistful. Almost gets lost in the moment, then snaps himself out of it.*

Frank?

SHAUN. Why d'yer mammy call you Pearl then?

PEARL. She called us Pearl and Ruby after the jewels she'd never be able to afford.

KENNY. FRANK!

FRANK *wakes with a jolt. They laugh.*

FRANK. Where's the fire?

KENNY. You wanna come and look at these LPs before close of play?

FRANK. LPs. LPs. Yes.

KENNY. Come now then, Frankie, or they're going in the bin.

FRANK. I'm coming I'm coming.

FRANK *goes past him and through the door leading upstairs.* KENNY *stops.*

KENNY (*to* FRANK). I'll follow you on.

KENNY *turns to the audience. Then, conspiratorially, he delivers the monologue directly to them.* PEARL *and* SHAUN *are unaware.*

Best night I've ever had in this pub? In twenty years of being landlord? You'll laugh. You'll think: Ooh, Kenny, you morbid cunt.

7th July 2005. 7:7.

First I heard was from Teddy, as I opened up. 'They got us, Ken.' Words stuck in his throat. Jameson's chaser with his breakfast pint – I joined him – rude not to. We switched on the news and left it on. That's a first. This is a sanctuary; I like to give people a break from ethnic cleansing and economic downturn. Give 'em balls and rackets instead.

The day was eerie, nervy. Regulars didn't sit in their usual spots. They all sat round that table over there. Watched.

People got closer; kinder, softer. The usual tightarses put their hands in their pockets – 'Same again, mate? Bag of nuts?' Some of the mums came in after school, said they just didn't want to go home. I put the kids in that corner, free crisps and Coke. Sugared off their tits, they were! Dad. Didn't have much to say for once. Mind you, looking back he was starting to show… Signs. (*Beat.*) After five they came streaming. The whole network shut down, people couldn't get home. This place was like a beacon. All the regulars from Churchill, couple of the old boys brought their wives up, we only see the likes of them at Christmas! They held hands at the bar – I remember. Pub filled with smoke. Cos you fucking could, then, couldn't ya? Orla and her school lot, there. (*Signals*.) She'd been crying. Little pink blotches like rosebuds at the top of her cheeks. What do you say to a class full of twelve-year-olds? When they ask you why someone's blowing up their country? Who'd be a teacher? Who'd be a kid?

So faces old and new. A few tears, few laughs. Some flashes of anger. But mainly it's just people being Nice To Each Other. In a Very British Way. And I'm in the centre of it all. With my girl there, and…

One of my school reports said: 'Kenneth appears to be out of step with the rest of the world.' I was eight. Eight! She was right though, Mrs Woolly, the fucking witch. But that night I was perfectly in sync. I felt like I had my arms around the whole pub. I felt like going into the street and tearing off my shirt and shouting FUCK YOU!

*He whispers a bit.*

Fuck you ISIS. Al-Qaeda. Whatever. You won't get us in here. WE ARE NOT AFRAID!

*Beat. The glory of the memory fades.*

But we are afraid. We are very afraid. Look outside – what a world! Death. Destruction. Disease… Divorce.

*He lifts his drink.*

A drink in your hand, sir? Your head in the sand, sir.

*He drinks. Savours it.*

Then we switched off the news.

KENNY *heads upstairs. There's a moment.* PEARL *starts wiping down the bar. It doesn't need it.*

SHAUN. Ken's just done that.

PEARL. He doesn't do it properly.

*Beat.*

Do you reckon this is it?

SHAUN *checks his watch, looks around the place.*

SHAUN. I reckon.

PEARL. You might be the last customer ever served in The Anchor.

SHAUN. An honour.

PEARL. End of an era, mate.

SHAUN. Yep. Who's gonna give us the lowdown on what I should be listening to? Or tell us I'm wearing shit trousers, like?

PEARL *starts giggling.*

PEARL. They weren't shit they were just...

SHAUN. Go on.

PEARL. Okay they were a bit shit.

*They laugh a bit.*

It was the pockets. They were... flappy!

SHAUN. What about these, not too flappy?

*He points to his trousers.*

PEARL. They're nice, actually.

SHAUN. A seal of approval! Without your advice I'm gonna become a proper old fart, you know that, don't ye?

PEARL. Never.

*Beat.*

SHAUN. Stick one in there, will ye?

*He passes his glass.*

Have one yourself if you like.

PEARL. I've got one.

SHAUN. Line 'em up. Let me buy you a drink for two years' excellent service.

PEARL. Go on then. Is it that long?

SHAUN. Aye. I've been here since Phase Two, so…

*Beat.*

Did you ask at The Hand and Flower?

PEARL. What about?

SHAUN. Bar work? I was having a wankerburger in there the other day –

PEARL (*gasps*). Traitor!

SHAUN. Come on, man, I was John Craven and I'm sick of instant noodles. Don't tell.

PEARL. I won't. Did you have The Stack?

SHAUN. With blue cheese and onion jam. It was class.

PEARL. Shhhhh!

SHAUN. Seen Frank in there you know!

PEARL. He likes the pulled pork.

*They laugh.*

SHAUN. Brian could use someone.

PEARL. I can't.

SHAUN. You're a cracking barmaid. It's a bloody hard job – dealing with us lot.

PEARL. I've had to run home twice tonight. (*Holds her phone up.*) This hasn't stopped ringing. Ken's good about it cos he knows Mum, but… Nah, it's gotta be something more… flexible.

*Beat.*

SHAUN. What about Avon? 'Avon calling'.

PEARL. Come on.

SHAUN. Why not?

PEARL. I don't think *I* could sell beauty products.

SHAUN. Aye you bloody well could.

PEARL. Really?

SHAUN. Yeah! A mate of me daughter's does it and she looks like she's been hit in the face with a pan.

PEARL. Oh.

SHAUN. What I mean is… You can do anything you set your mind to, Pearlie. You've just got that –

PEARL. What?

SHAUN. That spark.

*Beat.*

PEARL. Yeah?

*He nods and takes a large swig of his pint.*

I'm gonna do data entry.

SHAUN. Oh… right?

PEARL. I can do it all from home.

SHAUN. Can ya?

PEARL. Pack arrived this morning. Piece of piss.

*Beat.*

SHAUN. I said to Marie – our Lauren could do with a touch of what you have. Between you and me she's a fucking madam. Sittin' round the house all day painting her nails while Marie does everything for the babbie.

PEARL. You told your wife about me?

SHAUN. I just said, you know, how much you had to put up with.

PEARL. Did you tell her my name?

SHAUN. I think I just said the girl from The Anchor.

PEARL. Oh.

*She necks her pint and pours herself another.*

SHAUN. Thirsty?

PEARL. You know we were saying how amazing it would be to see Florence live?

SHAUN. With her Machine like?

PEARL. Yeah with her machine.

SHAUN. Definitely, man. That voice – it soars!

PEARL. Well she's playing at the Apollo! It's only down the road.

SHAUN. Ah great. You're going with your pals, are ye?

PEARL. No well I…

*Beat.*

I thought maybe we could go together.

SHAUN. Oh. Right…

PEARL. I mean I dunno if that's something you'd wanna do but I always think – I dunno, I always think you should go and see like live music with someone who gives a fuck you know someone who cares –

SHAUN. Yeah…

PEARL. About the music?

SHAUN. Yeah yeah well I mean / obviously like…

PEARL. I mean I think it would be a really good craic, you know, we can grab some food before we go, wankerburger even.

*He laughs a bit.*

What?

*Beat. He tries to find the right words.*

SHAUN. You don't wanna go to a pop concert with an old cunt like me, Pearlie.

PEARL. No, um yes, I mean I do… I – I don't mind.

*Pause. Mind racing.*

SHAUN. Okay.

PEARL. Yeah?

SHAUN. Yeah. Fuck it. Florence, here we come.

PEARL. Great!

SHAUN. Okay…

PEARL. Okay so the tickets sell out really really fast. Like super-fast.

SHAUN. Let's get on it / then

PEARL. So I bought two.

SHAUN. Oh – you – how much were they, love?

PEARL. That doesn't matter.

SHAUN. No come on –

PEARL. I wanted to buy them to say thanks.

SHAUN (*confused*). For what?

PEARL. Just um… being a mate.

SHAUN. I haven't done anything.

PEARL. It's my treat.

*Beat. He sighs.*

SHAUN. You're a… marvel. Drinks on me. All night.

PEARL. Okay. It's October the 15th.

SHAUN. Few weeks away.

PEARL. Do you want me to put it in your phone calendar?

SHAUN. No I think I can manage that. Blimey, what are you, me personal assistant now as well as me stylist?

*PEARL finds a newfound ballsiness that takes them into new territory. It doesn't quite land.*

PEARL. I'm a woman of many talents, Shaun.

*Beat. He looks at his phone.*

SHAUN. That's a Saturday, like.

PEARL. She's only doing one date.

SHAUN. I can't do a Saturday, love. I'll be back in Liverpool.

*Beat.*

PEARL. It's only one weekend.

SHAUN. What would I say to me family?

PEARL. Tell them the truth.

SHAUN. What? That I'm staying in London the weekend to go to a pop concert with a twenty-year-old lass?

PEARL. Tell them you're staying in London to see Florence and the Machine with a mate.

SHAUN. I… Listen, Pearl /

PEARL. Don't you want to?

SHAUN. It's not about whether I want to / or not

PEARL. Don't you want to spend time with me?

*Beat. Too direct.*

SHAUN. Fucking hell / this is a bit

PEARL. You know after tonight that's it?

*Beat.*

SHAUN. Pearlie.

PEARL (*snaps*). Forget it. I've had too much to drink. It's fine, I'll sell the tickets.

SHAUN. Okay or /

PEARL. I'll take a mate – I'll take Rubes.

SHAUN. Yeah I mean she'd love it wouldn't / she

BILBO *enters.*

PEARL. Fuck it I'll take Bilbo.

Bill, do you wanna see Florence?

BILBO. What?

PEARL. And the Machine?

BILBO. Ummm…

PEARL. 15th October. At the Apollo?

BILBO. Yeah whatever.

PEARL. Done. Sorted.

SHAUN. I would have liked to, / Pearl, it's just

PEARL. Let's not talk about it again.

*Beat. Fractious.* BILBO *sits down, heavy.*

SHAUN. Okay.

PEARL. Do you want a drink, 'Kevin'? We're getting pissed.

BILBO. Don't call me that.

SHAUN. That must have been a long fag. Superking, was it?

BILBO. I was ringing round my old foster homes.

PEARL. Any luck?

BILBO. Nah.

PEARL. What none of them can have you for a few days?

SHAUN. How many are there?

BILBO. Nine.

PEARL. What about the place you were at for years?

BILBO. We fell out.

PEARL. Why?

BILBO. Soon as I turned eighteen she kicked me out.

SHAUN. Why?

BILBO. She didn't realise she'd stop getting money for me.

SHAUN. That's awful, man.

BILBO *shrugs*

BILBO. Nah, Yaz was alright. She's gotta pay the bills. Spose I better go and pack. You alright to do close, Pearl?

PEARL. Yeah, babes.

SHAUN. Look I can't help with work, lad, but there's bound to be a bed at The Ferry for ya.

BILBO. That's like a… hostel. Isn't it? (*Shudders at the word.*)

PEARL. Yeah but not like a hostel hostel.

SHAUN. It's not The Ritz, but it's clean and comfortable. Well it's clean.

BILBO. Nah, you're alright.

SHAUN. What's in those two boxes should see you right for a couple of nights.

BILBO. I'm not up for sharing.

SHAUN. You don't have to be in a dorm, like. There's rooms with only two or three beds.

BILBO. You're alright, Shaun. Thanks.

SHAUN (*confused. A bit pissed off*). Suit yourself.

FRANK *and* KENNY *enter –* FRANK *carrying three LPs.*

FRANK. It's a splendid selection – I'm just sorry I can't take more. Joanie'll scold me. 'More old trash?' She'll say!

KENNY. Anyone been in for me, Shaun?

SHAUN. Sorry, mate.

BILBO. You alright, Ken?

KENNY *goes and stands at the door, looking out.* BILBO *watches him.*

PEARL. What you got, Frank?

FRANK. Nat King Cole – *Unforgettable*.

SHAUN (*to* KENNY). Didn't know you were into crooners?

KENNY. I'm not. They're Dad's.

SHAUN. Don't you wanna keep them?

KENNY. What for?

SHAUN. Sentimental… like.

*He keeps looking out the door.* FRANK *begins to put his coat on.*

KENNY. Nah. Fuck it.

FRANK. Lovely to have something of Lloyd's. He wouldn't have begrudged me, would he?

KENNY *doesn't respond.*

PEARL. Course he wouldn't.

BILBO. Ken? Shall I top you up?

*FRANK holds up the last record.*

FRANK. Tony Bennett! Something we agreed on!

*He looks at the track listing. Sings a bit:*

'I'm just a lucky so-and-so...' I used to sing that to Joanie when we were courting.

SHAUN. Bet you've never heard a record before, have you, Pearlie?

PEARL. Yeah. My cousin's got decks.

FRANK. Got what?

SHAUN. Turntables, Frank.

*Suddenly KENNY shouts.*

KENNY. FUCK IT.

*Beat.*

BILBO. Wassup?

KENNY. We're closed.

SHAUN. You kicking us out, Ken??

KENNY. Nope. I'm locking you in, mate.

*He disappears out of sight. Everyone looks at each other. We hear the sound of the doors being locked. KENNY appears.*

LOCK-IN!

SHAUN. The party was last night, / Ken.

KENNY. Fuck last night! Who'd be a landlord? People love you to your face but they slag you off behind ya back. You know someone's been running a *book* on what this place turns in to when it closes?

SHAUN. Wankers.                    FRANK. Terrible.

KENNY. They know I've been to hell and back! Well, fuck 'em. I don't wanna drink with Tommy Two-Phones and Weird Elaine. I've got you lot. Right?

SHAUN. Listen, I got an early start, / like.

FRANK. You know I must get back for Joanie.

KENNY. Come on!

BILBO. I'll stay with you, Ken.

KENNY. Finally: loyalty. Although you live here, so…

SHAUN. It's nothin' to do with loyalty, man, I'm still hanging from last night!

PEARL. I'll stay.

FRANK. But… did you say… free drinks? And a cab, was it?

KENNY. You're hardly other side of the world.

FRANK. Of course / it's just that

KENNY. YES we'll get you a sherbet too.

FRANK. I'm not going anywhere in an Uber.

KENNY. Course not! We'll get you a proper one.

FRANK. Well. If you put it like that… /

PEARL. Frank's staying out!

FRANK. First time for everything!

KENNY (*with genuine desperation*). Shaun?

> KENNY *is busy pouring shots for everyone.* SHAUN *catches* PEARL*'s eye. Beat. Decision.*

SHAUN. Fuck it. Who needs a liver anyway?

> *Everyone cheers.*

One condition: We do karaoke.

KENNY. Yes! Nice one, Shauny. (*Climbs on a chair.*) Right, gather round, ladies and gentlemen. Tonight, people, we are

going to drink to this pub, to The Anchor, to the last two
decades of my blood sweat tears and jizz –

PEARL/SHAUN. Jizz????

KENNY. – And drink it as dry as a fucking bone. No one puts
their hand in their pocket. When it's gone, it's gone!

*He raises his glass.*

ALL. When it's gone – it's gone!

*They cheer. Drink.*

*End of Act One.*

## ACT TWO

*We see a snapshot of each of their karaoke. Each little section could be punctuated with a shot smashed back, or a drink downed, with a change in position and a swap of the mic.*

*The opening bars of 'No No No (You Don't Love Me)' by Dawn Penn. KENNY comes running in from the toilet, doing his trousers up.*

KENNY. You started it, you prat!

BILBO. Sorry my finger slipped.

KENNY. Barely had time to put my dick away! Gimme that mic.

| | |
|---|---|
| KENNY *sings the beginning of the song.* | *All whoop and cheer and* KENNY *loves it – proper party atmosphere.* |
| | PEARL. Fuck – this is a proper summer song innit. |
| | BILBO. Ken loves this, man, it's his go-to number. |
| | SHAUN. Wonder why. |
| | BILBO. Shhh. |
| | FRANK. He sings it so convincingly. |
| KENNY *enjoys a little dance and they cheer.* | |
| Bilbo? | |
| | BILBO. Yes, mate? |
| Pour me a fucking pint, mate. | |

FRANK *sings Tony Bennett's version of 'Just a Lucky So And So'.*

*Intro of song plays.*

FRANK. When do I start?

Do I start now?

Oh – here, it's going red!

FRANK *sings.*

PEARL. When it goes red, Frank.

SHAUN. When it goes red.

BILBO. Isn't this the strippers' music?

KENNY. No, you knob!

BILBO. Yes it is. Go on, Frank get 'em off! Get 'em off.

PEARL. Ignore him, Frank. Sing it for Joanie!

BILBO *sings 'Fit But Don't You Know It' by The Streets.*

*Everyone enjoys* BILBO *enjoying his Streets rendition. He might actually be really fucking good at it. Or not. Everyone sings with* BILBO *and jumps up and down – having reached the peak of pissedness – it's probably downhill from here.*

KENNY *gets* BILBO *in an (affectionate) headlock.*

SHAUN *sings 'Wonderwall' by Oasis – more drunk.*

KENNY *and* BILBO *are deep in* Lord of the Rings *chat, loud over the music.*

FRANK *and* PEARL *watch* SHAUN.

KENNY. I mean Gandalf had his own reasons, do you know what I mean?

BILBO. Yeah.

SHAUN *puts his mic down. Irritated by* KENNY *and* BILBO *chatting and surprised by the fact he's getting a bit emotional.*

SHAUN. Ah fuck this.

KENNY. He *instinctively* knows Bilbo has to go with Thorin, yeah? Cos I think he knows on a *deep* level that it's Bilbo that's gotta get the ring and bring it to the Shire.

BILBO. Yeah. Yeah yeah.

PEARL. Don't stop. You were good!

SHAUN. Nah. Where's my beer?

*He sits and looks back at them. He talks to the audience.*

I don't do goodbyes.
Never have.
Marie winds me up about it: says I'm
Hard on the outside, but soft as shite in the middle.

*He looks at them. Sniffs.*

Nah.
I could walk out of here tonight and never look back.
And I'd count my blessings.
A house: mortgaged to the hilt, but in my name.
A wife – who's got heart
and humour and
Kids, Lauren: lost and stroppy.
But mine.

And Luke: First of our lot to go to uni.
York. Sociology. He's a changer.
A grandson. Archie.
Doesn't seem to warm to his granddad.
Every weekend feels like we're starting all over again.
But that's okay.
It's A Life.
And yes I work me fingers to the bone.
Yes I graft and sweat and lift and haul
Away all week, slummin' it
But that's okay.
We eat well, we drink well, We Live Well.
Usual takeaway from the usual Chinese
Usual hotel at the usual resort
Not enough to live it up – tear it up
But just enough to taste
the finer things in life.

BILBO, FRANK *and* KENNY *begin to chant: 'Pearlie!*
*Pearlie! Pearlie! Pearlie!' PEARL is convinced, takes the*
*mic. He watches for a moment. The intro to 'Ain't Nobody'*
*by Chaka Khan.*

And then...
Years spill into decades
Youth falls away and seems
A silly dream
A cartoon
Life flows past you, over you, through you
Punctuated by holidays, and weddings and christenings and
funerals
And before you know it,
You've more behind you than before you
That came quick, you think
But that's okay.
You're starting the slow wind-down.
Knowing you and yours are fed and watered.
Knowing you love and are loved
Knowing you have just enough
Of what you want.

Of what you need.
And that's okay.

*Pause.*

Until someone makes you a playlist

PEARL *sings a few lines from 'Ain't Nobody'.*

*Beat.*

And you pretend you haven't listened to it yet.
But the truth is you've listened to every fucking song over
and over and over
And when you look in the mirror you see
A cocksure lad
And a silly aul man
You're hot and dizzy and grumpy
and forlorn and stupid and ecstatic
and sick
With the thought of it
With the thought of her
And when you're near her
Fuck.
You could be eighteen again
All hair gel and hard-ons
All stonewashed jeans
And secret dreams
Sinking your second pint at the beginning of a night
Where anything is possible.

*Her eyes fix his. It's too much. He heads to the toilet.
Karaoke fades. The others drift. PEARL is left holding the
mic, watching the direction that SHAUN left.*

KENNY *is sitting with his feet up at one of the tables.*

BILBO. You alright, Ken?

KENNY. Pukka. Course I am. Wanna sit?

*Beat. He does. KENNY looks at him.*

Well it's been an honour and a privilege, young man.

BILBO. Cheers. (*Beat.*) You know… tomorrow?

KENNY. I do know 'Tomorrow'. Only too well. It's galloping towards me like a fucking rabid white horse foaming at the mouth. With… wings… On fire.

BILBO. Right.

BILBO. Well, thing is /

KENNY. Need a lift? Mr Walker can give you a lift in his works van. After six.

BILBO. It's not that.

KENNY. What is it then?

BILBO. I might have a bit of a problem. With… somewhere to stay.

KENNY. You said you were all / sorted

BILBO. It's just happened.

*Beat.* KENNY *sighs.*

KENNY. Alright.

BILBO (*lighting up*). What, you mean…

KENNY *reaching into his pocket, getting his little wodge of notes out.*

KENNY. I gave Pearl a drink, only fair that / I

BILBO. Nah it's not that. *You* need that. I just – /

KENNY. You want me to go council offices with you?

BILBO. I…

KENNY. Alright. But after eleven or I'll still be pissed.

BILBO. No I don't wanna go there, Ken.

KENNY. You've *gotta* go. The brewery has made you homeless, Bill. Or Jarvis has.

BILBO. Thing is I / don't think that –

KENNY. You're vulnerable. Cos of – you know. Problems. (*Vaguely gestures his head.*)

BILBO. Ken!

KENNY. You gotta say these things, matey! At least that'll get you a hostel.

*Beat. The word 'hostel' pricks something chilling in* BILBO.

BILBO. I don't wanna do that, Ken.

KENNY. Well… /

BILBO (*louder, an edge of panic*). I don't wanna go to a hostel like before.

KENNY. Well, beggars, choosers, Bill. You know what I mean?

BILBO. I can't. I can't!

*Others look over.* KENNY *stands up – a bit embarrassed at* BILBO*'s outburst.*

KENNY (*standing up*). You wanted my advice? That's it! You don't wanna fucking take it that's your lookout.

KENNY *goes to the bar, pours himself a drink, downs it, leaving* BILBO *wrestling with his situation.* PEARL *has been watching. She walks round the bar and addresses* KENNY.

PEARL. Oi, you. Breathe on me.

KENNY. What? No.

PEARL *grabs the glass and sniffs it.*

PEARL. Fuck's sake!

KENNY. Hang on /

FRANK. Not the firewater?

PEARL. Yep!

PEARL *holds up a bottle of Johnnie Walker Red Label.*

FRANK. Oh, Kenneth.

SHAUN. Come on, Pearl, he's a grown man.

KENNY. Thank you, Shaun.

PEARL. He's a dick on this stuff!

KENNY. Can we stop talking about me like I'm not here?

PEARL. Alright – you're a dick on this stuff!

FRANK. It sends you round the / twist.

KENNY. OI OI OI! Thank you! It's my last night as the landlord of my own pub. I know my limits. Tonight I'm making the decisions. Alright?

SHAUN. Got it, Ken.

*Beat.*

Pearl.

PEARL. Alright.

FRANK. Very well.

KENNY. Thank you. Shaun?

*He offers him a drink of Scotch.*

SHAUN. Not for me. Early start.

KENNY. Oh have a drink, you Northern Irish twat.

*Beat.*

SHAUN. Well when you put it like that.

PEARL. Shaun!

KENNY. Frankie?

FRANK. Well if you insist I / suppose I

PEARL. Frank! God. Gimme one then.

KENNY. Ha! (*Pours for her.*) Mr Baggins?

BILBO *looks over, gives a small smile.*

*They gather around* KENNY *as he pours large measures of whisky.* BILBO *drinks.*

Tasting notes, Mr Baggins?

BILBO *swills the whisky around his mouth.*

BILBO. Pretty earthy, Ken.

KENNY. Yep.

BILBO. With a touch of fucking... figs?

KENNY. Nice one.

BILBO. And the merest suggestion of –

*He sips again.*

Cowboy's nutsack!

KENNY. Bingo! Fucking love this boy!

*The music, which has been playing on shuffle, changes to 'Liquidator' by The Harry J Allstars.*

PEARL. Shhh. Listen!

FRANK. Not the birds yet, is it? (*Puts his hands over ears.*) Oh I hate / the bloody birds.

PEARL. Nah. Bill – turn it up!

*She does.*

Remember?

BILBO. My first week here.

FRANK. A great night in the history of great nights.

SHAUN. I'm in the fucking dark here like. lads...

KENNY. Champions League Final 2012, right, Bill?

BILBO. Yeah.

SHAUN. Oh yeah... / yeah

KENNY. What a fucking drama! /

BILBO. I turned up and the place is rammed. A *sea* of blue. Flags and banners and /

KENNY. This turnip turns up in a red T-shirt.

SHAUN. Oh, / Dildo, man...

*They laugh.*

PEARL. Oh my GOD / yeah!

BILBO. I didn't know, did I?

KENNY. Lucky I had a spare strip, made him change out the back.

BILBO. It was too bloody small /

PEARL. Yeah it looked like a crop-top!

SHAUN. Ha brilliant /

BILBO. And Northern Irish Carol done a massive buffet, and you let me have a plate before I started. I'm telling you, man, I hadn't eaten properly for three days. Those vol-au-vents were amazing.

PEARL. Northern Irish Carol does smash a vol-au-vent /

FRANK. Like little works of art. /

BILBO. The place was *wired*. Tense.

KENNY. Cos we were there by the skin of our teeth – we were struggling /

PEARL. Yeah we shouldn't have been there /

SHAUN. No you bloody shouldn't – not with that cunt Terry on your team.

PEARL. Shhhh

SHAUN. Sorry, Frank.

KENNY. Yeah well he was suspended, / wasn't he?

SHAUN. Hang on, Pearl shouldn't have been working, she was sixteen!

PEARL. I know, I was in with Mum, she was sneaking me Breezers.

KENNY. We didn't even sell Breezers!

PEARL. I know! /

SHAUN. Oops! /

FRANK. Went behind in the last ten minutes, didn't we? /

KENNY. Eighty-third. Bayern Munich fucking bossed it. /

SHAUN. As you would expect.

BILBO. I kept messing up. Getting orders wrong. I spilt a pint down someone mental. Bob, was it?

KENNY. It was Fingers.

PEARL. Oh shit yeah!

BILBO. He was not happy.

SHAUN. Why's he called Fingers?

PEARL/KENNY. Cos he's got no thumbs.

SHAUN (*laughing*). Jesus Christ.

PEARL. He's fucking mental. Ken, show him the cue.

KENNY *gets a broken and splintered half pool cue down from above the bar. Wafts it near* SHAUN*'s face.*

SHAUN. Careful, man, that's lethal.

PEARL. Broke it over his knee like it was a twig.

SHAUN. Why?

KENNY. Cos he tried to play fucking pool with it!

PEARL *and* BILBO *mime trying to play pool with no thumbs. They laugh.*

FRANK. Anyway…

KENNY (*to SHAUN*). It was starting to look like we'd fucked it.

BILBO. Everyone was shouting, chanting, singing at the screen and I remember thinking it was like they could fucking hear us; all the way in Germany. Cos right at the end /

PEARL. Drogba scored!

KENNY. Fucking legend!

BILBO. And the place just fucking EXPLODED /

KENNY. ERUPTED /

SHAUN. I'm not surprised, like /

BILBO. That's when this song come on. People went nuts, jumping and dancing and I think there was a Conga at one point.

FRANK *puts his hand up.*

FRANK. I started that.

BILBO. Men were cuddling and there were all kiddies up on shoulders – and then –

KENNY. We went to extra time, then we got to penalties.

PEARL. Drogba steps up to take the winning penalty, silence /

FRANK. Could have heard a mouse fart.

KENNY. And he SMASHES IT. /

KENNY *and* PEARL *and* FRANK *begin singing under* BILBO's *next section:*

'*Carefree – wherever we may be*
*We are the famous CFC*
*And we don't give a fuck whoever you may be*
*Cos we are the famous CFC*'

BILBO. And it went MENTAL. This whole bit here was like a fucking mosh pit. People were crying, kids were jumping off the walls outside. /

KENNY. Some of the lads ran out and got topless in the street – waved their T-shirts like flags –

PEARL. Ha! Gross.

BILBO. They picked me up at one point and put me on their shoulders and I'm covered in beer and sweat and I thought 'This. Is. Fucking... AMAZING.'

*Everyone laughs.*

KENNY. Classic /

FRANK. A great night /

PEARL. Yeah.

SHAUN. Sounds class, like.

*They laugh.* BILBO *doesn't mind.*

KENNY. We've had some good times... Haven't we?

BILBO/PEARL. Yeah.            SHAUN. We have, Ken.

FRANK. Mmm.

*The music fades. The memory fades.*

KENNY. Pints.

*'Goodbye My Lover' by James Blunt comes on.*

PEARL. How can you drink / beer now?

FRANK. I'll join you in a pint, / Ken.

SHAUN. Yeah I'll have one with me Scotch. (*Holds his glass of Scotch up.*) What's the opposite of a chaser?

PEARL. A... leader?

SHAUN. Foster's leader for me, Ken. Ken?

*They look over at* KENNY *who is frozen, head bowed over the pump.*

FRANK. Kenneth?

*Beat.* KENNY*'s voice cracks.*

KENNY. Finished.

SHAUN. Oh, right well...

*Pause. No one moves.*

KENNY. Finished.

*KENNY quietly begins to cry. Puts his hand on the bar to steady himself.*

*PEARL looks at BILBO.*

PEARL *(quietly)*. When it's gone it's gone.

*He sobs, quietly at first. Then it becomes more guttural – more howl-like. It's been a long time coming. The rest are horrified, panicked – they make small moves towards him, look at each other, wide-eyed – shrug, shake heads.*

PEARL. Kenny?

SHAUN. Talk to us, man.

KENNY *(through sobs)*. Can someone –

PEARL. Go / on.

FRANK. What can we do?

KENNY *(sobbing more)*. Can someone –

BILBO. Ken?

PEARL. What do you need mate? /

KENNY. Can someone TURN THAT CUNT OFF?

SHAUN. Who's put / James Blunt on, fuck's sake?

PEARL. Was that you, Bill, you / tool?

BILBO. It's on shuffle!

FRANK. Let's turn it off.

*BILBO runs over to the laptop and shuts it. There's silence and stillness, except for KENNY crying. BILBO makes a small move towards the bar but stops, not equipped for this. FRANK stands. SHAUN drinks his Scotch. PEARL makes the most dynamic movement and goes over, sits up on the bar and puts her hand on his shoulder.* KENNY *looks up, looks at them.*

KENNY. I – I hope –

PEARL. What?

> KENNY *takes* PEARL *and* BILBO *in.*

KENNY. I hope that… it's easier for you two. When you're young you think life is going to be…

FRANK. Different.

KENNY. Yeah. I'm not saying it's gonna be all… I mean you two you've had enough already to…

FRANK. Yes they have.

KENNY. I just mean… I would have liked to have done some more stuff. Different stuff. In my life.

*Beat. Confusion.*

SHAUN. What do ya mean, like hang gliding or a bungee jump?

KENNY. NO! I mean – when Bridgette was born, Frank, were you there?

FRANK. No I was here.

KENNY. What about you, Shaun – were you there with your two?

SHAUN. Not with Lauren, I was on the rigs then. But with our Luke I was, yeah.

KENNY. And – you saw it?

SHAUN. I didn't go down the business end, like.

KENNY. Why not?

SHAUN. Well, it's a bit like watching your favourite pub burn down.

PEARL (*laughing*). Ugh, Shaun.

KENNY. But was it beautiful?

SHAUN. Well when they'd cleaned him up a bit.

*Beat. He concedes. Enjoys the memory.*

Aye it was... beautiful, like.

KENNY. I would have liked to have done that. Me and Orla we... We had a couple of disasters.

FRANK. I remember. Very sad, Ken.

SHAUN. You're talking like your life's over.

KENNY. I'm fifty this year. /

SHAUN. I'm looking forward to fifty.

KENNY. Says the married man with two kids and a house.

SHAUN. But don't you feel more comfortable in your own skin?

KENNY. What, in this?

*He indicates his own skin.*

PEARL. Come on you, Ken, you could find the woman of your dreams in Chatham.

KENNY. Have you ever been to Chatham?

SHAUN. She's right. You never know what's round the corner, man.

*He briefly catches eyes with* PEARL. *How true.* KENNY *shakes his head. He's pissed.*

KENNY. I've never had any luck with women. Always been too soft. When I was ten I got to dance with Hayley Bibberton at the Christmas disco. She smelt like apples and she was the first girl in our year to get breasts. There we are, swaying to Hot Chocolate, and we're pressed up against each other – you know – and I can feel the outline of her bra – fuck it was like a foreign country, lads!

PEARL. That is minging, Ken /

KENNY (*shouts*). What? I was a sexual being once, you know!

PEARL. Alright keep your / hair on!

KENNY. I've not always been the sexless aberration you see before you / now!

SHAUN. Steady on, man /

KENNY. Well. I'm telling a fucking story here! Aren't I, Frank?

FRANK. You certainly are.

KENNY. We're dancing, like, *pressed*. And my little mate Trevor was standing about a foot away from me looking green, you know, cos he loved Hayley too. All the boys did. But Trev was my bestest pal in all the world. And he keeps whispering – just so I can hear: 'Such a lucky sausage, Kenny. *Such* a lucky sausage' over and over. '*Such* a lucky sausage.' So what d'you think I did?

PEARL. Punched him in the face?

KENNY. I *gave* Hayley to him. I let them dance and I watched. And that's what I did with *Orla*. I welcomed that man into my pub. I got those wanky craft ales in for him and I showed the fucking rugby for him. I gave her to him on a plate.

PEARL *has grown irritated with all this.*

PEARL. You '*gave*' him Hayley, you '*gave*' him Orla. They weren't household pets!

KENNY. It's the story of my life. Just like Jason fucking Jarvis taking my beloved pub.

PEARL. It's not the same. The pub – it's just business. Hayley who smelt of apples – you were a little snotty kid. And Orla fell in love with Neil the PE teacher.

KENNY. Don't say his NAME!

PEARL. You've gotta accept it, / Kenny

KENNY (*with venom*). NEEEIIIILLLLLL!

PEARL. It happens. It's over. Move on.

*He shakes his head. Slumps down in a chair.*

KENNY. Never. Never never never never.

*Beat.* KENNY *puts his head in his hands.* PEARL *looks to*
FRANK *and* SHAUN. SHAUN *beckons her over: give*
KENNY *some space.* BILBO *watches* KENNY. *Grabs the*
*whisky bottle. Two glasses. After a few moments he goes and*
*pulls up a stool next to him. He thinks about it. Then he pats*
*him on the arm tentatively. He pours them a drink.*

BILBO. Ken? It's alright, Ken.

KENNY *takes the drink.* BILBO *steels himself for a few*
*moments. Takes a deep breath.*

I know that this might sound like totally fucking weird or
whatever. But I was thinking – I was thinking about you
moving to Chatham and the pub closing down and
everything and I was thinking about… I guess I was…
Sounds stupid… But I was thinking…

*He's started so he has to finish.*

Why don't I come with you?

KENNY *looks at him, blank-faced.*

To… Chatham.

*Pause.* KENNY *just looks at* BILBO.

I mean – I mean I don't really have anywhere to go or
anything to do, and you don't really – I mean – you've got
stuff to *do* obviously but – but –

*He's floundering*

You are – you've been – like a *significant person* in my life,
Kenny. Like a… model. A role model.

*A little laugh escapes from* KENNY.

KENNY. Poor cunt.

BILBO (*confused*). I could be your call-over partner? Frank
was your dad's call-over partner when they were doing The

Knowledge. I could do all the runs with you. I could sleep on the floor.

*Beat.*

Do all the washing up.

KENNY. Oh, Bill.

BILBO. What do you reckon?

KENNY. No.

BILBO. No?

KENNY. NO! No! Course you can't. Course you can't.

*Beat.*

BILBO. I'm in a bit of a... pickle.

KENNY (*animated suddenly*). A PICKLE? A PICKLE? There's some Pilgrim's Choice in the fridge upstairs. Go and make yourself a sandwich.

BILBO. I just / mean

KENNY (*to the others*). What's he trying to do to me?
(*To* BILBO.) What do you reckon this is? Some bromance. Romcom. When Harry met fucking... Larry.

BILBO. Just temporary / like

KENNY. This is life, Bilbo! You just gotta fucking deal with it.

BILBO. I'm scared. About what's gonna /

KENNY (*lashing out*). Look – I'm not ya dad! I'm not your foster parent. I'm not your brother; I'm not your fucking... social worker. Right?

BILBO. No you're my mate.

KENNY. I'm your boss! (*Checks his watch.*) Or I WAS. So just... fuck the fuck off, yeah?

PEARL. What's going on?

KENNY. He's not my responsibility, Pearl. He works here and he lives here. Just cos we got a shared love of Honey Nut

Cheerios and *Lord of the* fucking *Rings* don't mean we're gonna ride off into the Medway sunset together. You got that?

PEARL. Why d'you have to shout at him?

BILBO (*distraught*). I only meant for a little while! (*To* PEARL.) I only wanted to stay with him for a little / while!

PEARL. Alright, Bill.

KENNY. I'm moving on I'm moving up, I don't want any lame ducks.

FRANK. Kenneth!

KENNY. Well, look at him. He's a snivelling mess.

BILBO *stands*.

BILBO. You couldn't run this place without me!

KENNY. That's a joke. Pearl maybe.

BILBO. You'd be fucked without me. You said it yourself!

KENNY. Fucked without *you*?? Do me a lemon. Do you remember the first time we met?

BILBO. Yeah for the interview.

KENNY. HA. 'INTERVIEW.'

PEARL. Don't, / Ken.

KENNY. EH ERR. (*i.e.* Family Fortunes *wrong-answer sound effect*.) Wrong. You used to beg outside my pub, remember? You used to come round here all barefoot, talking to yourself –

BILBO. No I didn't /

KENNY. Playing Bruno Mars out loud on your phone, picking up dog-ends off the pavement /

BILBO. Pearl? /

PEARL. That's / enough!

KENNY. 'Spare a cigarette? Spare ten pee? Spare a cigarette?' On day release from the nuthouse!

BILBO. It's not a nuthouse.

*KENNY grabs his whisky and swigs from the bottle.*

KENNY (*to* SHAUN). Sorry. 'Secure mental health' unit.

PEARL. STOP / IT

BILBO. Then why d'ya give me the job then if I was so shit?

KENNY. As a favour!

BILBO. To who?

KENNY. Your social worker! She was a mate of Orla's. I'd have done anything to get her to shag me again.

BILBO. Piss off, old man!

KENNY. You're an embarrassment.

BILBO. You can talk.

KENNY. Come on then, what you got, Einstein?

BILBO. What about Paddy's Day?

PEARL. Oh God not / this.

KENNY. What about it?

BILBO. You were a mess!

KENNY (*to* SHAUN *and* FRANKIE). My Irish wife left me on Paddy's Day – so once a year, when it comes round, if I wanna pass out in my own bog that's my prerogative – right?

BILBO (*shouting*). Yeah but not if me and Pearl have to clean the shit off you!

*Stunned silence. KENNY looks to PEARL, back to BILBO – then starts to sing quite aggressively at them.*

KENNY *sings 'Love Changes Everything' from the musical* Aspects of Love.

*He gets louder as the song goes on.*

PEARL. What the fuck's he doing?

SHAUN. Right, get your shit together, yous, we're leaving.

FRANK. He's lost the / plot

*They start to collect coats and bags and* KENNY *continues to sing at them, following them.*

SHAUN. You too, Bilbo.

BILBO. I fucking live here.

PEARL. We'll sort something for you tonight, mate. Frank, get your hat.

FRANK. All of this palaver /

*They have got to the door and* KENNY *is in front of them, holding both arms out, blocking the door.*

SHAUN *laughs at him.*

KENNY *struggles to reach a high note and –*

*In one movement he grabs the splintered cue from above the bar and holds it out threateningly, eyes ablaze.*

SHAUN. Get real, man!

SHAUN. Whoa, hang on.

PEARL. What the fuck?

KENNY. Get back from the door.

*Beat. Tension.*

FRANK. Drop the cue, Kenneth!

BILBO. Now who's mental!

*He lurches towards them.*

SHAUN. Whoa calm down.          PEARL. Shut it, Bill.
                                Dickhead.

BILBO. Alright sorry!

FRANK. He wouldn't hurt us.

KENNY. Try me.

FRANK. He's no action hero.

*Beat. Breathless. KENNY concedes – they're right. Instead
he jerkily moves the cue closer to his own neck.*

SHAUN. No!          BILBO. Fuck!          PEARL. Kenny,
                                          don't!

KENNY. Nervous, aren't you, very very nervous?

*He sort of drives them back. He's taken on an impish quality.
Unnerving.*

SIT DOWN. HAVE A DRINK. (*Beat.*) ENJOY
YOURSELVES.

*Beat. No one moves. He moves the cue an inch closer to his
neck, and they all sit down. He keeps on his feet, mobile,
possibly pacing around them.*

That song was from her favourite musical. I took her to see
it. It was shit. I hate the theatre. It's just like the cinema but
with more cunts.

SHAUN. Kenny, you're a twisted fuck.

KENNY. SHAUN SPEAKS! The perfect man. Married twenty
years right?

SHAUN. Twenty-seven.

KENNY. Couple of kids, a grandson! Nice wife, bit rough
around the edges but –

SHAUN (*standing*). You fucking what /

KENNY *lurches the cue towards them and he sits.*

KENNY. What a life to squander!

SHAUN. Squander!?

KENNY. Sniffing around my bar staff like some old / lecherous bastard

SHAUN. What are you talking about, man?

KENNY. I've seen the looks, the winks, the giggles.

BILBO. What giggles?

KENNY. All the free Stellas. Under my nose. While this place was going down the pan. Looks like you're more like your mum than we thought, Pearl!

PEARL. I'll kill him!

PEARL *gets up and is ready to punch* KENNY *out until* FRANK *gets between them.*

FRANK. Now that's ENOUGH! Please. Come on, Pearl!

PEARL. He's a waste of fucking space.

PEARL *backs off reluctantly.*

KENNY. Frankie. My dad's bestest mate!

FRANK *turns on him, furious.*

FRANK. Look at yourself, Kenneth. You've abused this poor boy.

BILBO. Thanks but I'm not a / boy

FRANK. He's opened his heart to you. He's been very loyal. We all have. Even if Shaun and Pearl were having it off every time your back's turned /

PEARL. Steady on, / Frank.        SHAUN. Hang on there.

FRANK. They don't deserve to be treated like this.

KENNY. I'm fucking finished, Frankie.

FRANK. With what?

KENNY. People.

FRANK. Oh for goodness' / sake.

KENNY. All the beautiful people in my life are gone. Mum. Orla. (*Beat.*) Dad. I can see him, sitting there. Putting the world to rights. People respected him. Loved him. Life's a bastard. Why do they take all the / beautiful people??

FRANK. Oh, bollocks.

KENNY. What?

FRANK. Yes, I can see him sitting there. Nine pints in. Slurring his words and chewing the ear off some poor unsuspecting sod /

KENNY. My dad was a Good Man.

FRANK. I'm not suggesting he wasn't –

KENNY. And he loved me! He was proud of me!

FRANK. He thought you were a piss artist like him. And he was right.

*Beat. Hush.*

You're living in a dream world.

KENNY. That's rich coming from you.

FRANK. You look ridiculous, Kenneth.

KENNY. Your whole life's a fantasy, mate.

FRANK. Oh what are you on about?

KENNY. You know.

FRANK. Someone should make this man a strong black coffee.

SHAUN. That's not a bad idea. Bilbo –

KENNY. Don't MOVE! Frankie /

PEARL. Leave Frank alone.

FRANK. I'd like to go home now.

KENNY. Joanie waiting up, is she?

FRANK. I'd like to leave right now, Kenneth.

SHAUN. She'll be worried – let him go.

KENNY. Ever met Joanie?

SHAUN. No. So?

FRANK. I feel sick. I want to go to the toilet.

KENNY. No one leaves this room /

FRANK (*a thundering shout*). I NEED TO GO TO THE LOO! LET ME GO!

*Beat. This shakes* KENNY.

SHAUN. Kenny. Look at yourself. He's an old man.

*It is as though* KENNY *wakes up. He drops the cue. Sits. Head in hands.*

FRANK *goes to the toilet.* PEARL *takes control of the situation. Pulls a chair up in front of* KENNY. *Taps him on the shoulder, firmly. He looks her in the eye. It hurts.*

PEARL. What gives?

KENNY. Don't wanna talk about it.

PEARL. No no no. You don't get to do that! TELL US.

*Beat.* KENNY *looks around at the faces staring intently at him.*

KENNY. Joanie's dead.

*Stunned pause.*

PEARL. What?

SHAUN. That's ridiculous. You're / sick.

PEARL. You're lying.

KENNY. I'm not.

PEARL. How do you know?

KENNY. About four years ago, this was: we didn't see Frank
for best part of a week. I went up there, in the end. No sign.
Couple of days later I bumped into – what's-his-name...
Warren! Who used to go out with Frank's girl Bridgette. And
he told me then. She had a multiple stroke.

*Beat.*

PEARL. Oh my God.

SHAUN. So was Frank just... home alone?

KENNY. He was in Cork scattering her ashes.

*Beat.*

PEARL. And when he got back?

KENNY. Just walked in one day. Never mentioned it. We just...
carried on.

SHAUN. As you do.

KENNY. Yes you do, as it goes, I wouldn't expect you to
understand.

PEARL. Poor Frank.

KENNY. Then one day he just starts talking about Joan. What
she's cooked him. What she's moaning about. Like nothing's
happened.

SHAUN. And Bridgette?

KENNY. She lives in Spain or something. Only comes over at
Christmas.

BILBO. Why didn't you tell us, Ken?

KENNY. Not my place, boy. A landlord's the keeper of secrets.
The layman's /

PEARL (*angrily*). You're not keeping these secrets too well
now, are you, mate?

KENNY (*angrily*). Yeah well that's cos...

*It sinks in. Defeat.*

I'm not a pub landlord any more.

*He necks from the bottle. Despair. The sound of the loo flushing. FRANK comes in from the toilet. Everyone looks at FRANK. Silence.*

FRANK. What you all staring at?

PEARL. You alright, Frank?

FRANK (*suspicious*). Fine.

KENNY. Do you want a drink, Frankie?

FRANK. No. Thank you. I've had quite enough.

KENNY. I'm sorry I went / a bit

FRANK. Could somebody pass my hat?

KENNY. I'm sorry everyone, / I –

BILBO. I got it for ya.

KENNY. Fucked up.

SHAUN. Why don't you come and sit down?

FRANK. No. Must get home. See my wife. (*Looks at them intently – trying to work out what they know.*) I'm too old for this… silly buggers.

BILBO *stands. He's dynamic.*

BILBO. Don't go, Frank.

FRANK. Got to. Don't be silly.

SHAUN. What about that cab then?

FRANK. No. Need the air. Right, see you tomorrow.

*Beat. He makes towards the door.*

SHAUN. Er… Frank, mate /

FRANK. Yes?

KENNY. You won't.

FRANK. What?

KENNY. See us. Tonight's. The last night innit?

FRANK. Last...

*He looks around. The enormity dawns on* FRANK. *Hits him.*

Oh. Yes.

*He hovers, not knowing quite what to do.* PEARL *walks to him, gives him a big big hug.*

Gosh.

*She puts his hat on his head. He smiles and nods to her. He walks towards the door. It's painful to watch. As he gets to the door he stumbles and leans to one side, looking like he might collapse.*

| PEARL. Frank! | KENNY. Catch him. Someone! | SHAUN. Quick quick. |
|---|---|---|

BILBO *runs to* FRANK *and grabs his arm, hoists him up.*

BILBO. I got him. I got you, Frank.

SHAUN. See him home, will you?

BILBO. Yeah yeah. I got this. Pearl, pass my phone.

PEARL (*looking behind the bar*). Can't see it.

BILBO. Shaun, help me out here.

SHAUN *goes to support* FRANK *while* BILBO *darts across to the bar to get his phone.*

FRANK. What a load of... silly nonsense. I'm alright. I'm alright!

*On the way back to* FRANK, KENNY *grabs* BILBO.

KENNY. Bilbo. Come here.

*He pulls* BILBO *so he is face to face with him. He kisses him really tenderly on the head.* BILBO *is taken aback.*

Prince.

BILBO *nods. Goes to* FRANK.

PEARL. Bill. Text me.

BILBO. Yeah.

*They exit.* SHAUN, KENNY *and* PEARL *left in the aftermath. They eye each other, awkwardly, shyly, ashamed – not knowing what to say.*

*They talk to the audience.*

PEARL. It's 3 a.m.

KENNY. It's too late.

BILBO. Must be half-two? Or three?

SHAUN. It's later than I want it to be. Too late to be awake now with a 7 a.m. start.

PEARL. Just the three of us left.

BILBO. Me and Frank tramp the pavements. Don't say a word. We bump into parked cars and trip over kerbs.

SHAUN. Kenny necks from the bottle and is silent.

BILBO. There's a chill in the air. Summer is dying. For the first time in months. I can see my breath.

PEARL. Frank's story shakes me. Wakes me up.
Suddenly I sense time rushing by
really fucking quickly.

FRANK. It's that quiet time, when night is most severe.
And the sky couldn't be more clear or more black
Dawn hasn't crept in at the edges yet
It's like the sky has swallowed up all the stars.

PEARL. I know what I want.

KENNY. Once upon a time there was this giant

PEARL. I open the laptop

SHAUN. She puts on the playlist

KENNY. Who lived at the top of this great big fuck-off
   beanstalk.

FRANK. I like to count the stars, usually
   pick out the Plough
   And Polaris
   But tonight I count the lights instead
   Coming from windows, flats and houses,
   Who's is up at this ungodly hour?
   I invent little stories about their lives.

BILBO. Frank shuffles
   mutters under his breath
   like he's counting
   Or praying
   or something.

SHAUN. I go to the pisser
   I look in the mirror –
   and I see
   A cocksure lad
   And a silly aul man.

FRANK. Bedroom lights on in Tachbrook!
   Won't go to sleep on a lovers' tiff?
   Quite right too
   We never did
   We never do.

KENNY. This giant had some very nice things like a beautiful
   wife and some golden fucking eggs and a golden fucking
   goose and a magic harp or some such shit.

PEARL. Kenny's dead to the world. Dreaming some horrible
   dream.

SHAUN. We stand there looking at each other and there's
   a moment when it feels like something's gonna happen.

   But I grab my bag.

PEARL. I think you're gorgeous.

*Beat. He is shocked at the directness.*

SHAUN. Come on, Pearl.

PEARL. What?

SHAUN. ...Justin Bieber is gorgeous.

PEARL *thinks this is fucking ridiculous.*

PEARL. He's a fucking embryo!

SHAUN. Well, I don't know what you girls like.

PEARL. Yes you do.

KENNY. The harp used to play without being touched. Cos the giant was a piss artist and he would have broken the strings.

FRANK. Lupus street: A flat-screen TV /

KENNY. Then one day this cunt called Jack legs it up the beanstalk and steals away the giant's wife. /

FRANK. Lights the whole room /

KENNY. The giant would like to rip out his eyes and piss on his brain but he's never been 'tough' like that. /

FRANK. And a man sits alone. /

KENNY. And he thinks he was probably never good enough for her anyway.

FRANK. That could be any one of a thousand stories.
A thousand stories in the city!

SHAUN. Kenny's out for the count eh?

PEARL. Don't change the subject.

SHAUN. I'm not /

PEARL. Do you like me?

SHAUN. Of course I do.

PEARL. I know I'm not fit, like – really attractive – or anything /

SHAUN. What? You're wrong. You're very… It's just.

PEARL. What?

KENNY. So the giant rips the strings from the harp and he wrings the neck of the goose and he lobs the eggs against the wall then he just sits around the house in his underpants, covered with feathers and runny egg.

SHAUN. Well, where does this end, Pearl? Where do you see this going?

*Beat.* PEARL *realises with a laugh.*

PEARL. Oh I get it! You think *I* think you're gonna leave your wife. And we get a flat. Have kiddies and a fucking cat. Ride off into the sunset. (*To the audience.*) Aren't men stupid sometimes? (*Back to* SHAUN.) None of you idiots ever say what you really want! So that's what I'm doing. *This* is what I want.

SHAUN. Jesus…

PEARL. Tell me what you're thinking. Right now.

SHAUN. Nothing.

PEARL. Don't be a bell-end.

SHAUN. Okay. Okay. I'm thinking.

*Beat*

About your skin.

KENNY. Then he gets his axe and chops down the beanstalk. So no one can get up there again. (*Beat.*) Mind you that means he can't get down either. And I spose that means… Oh fuck it. I don't know where I'm going with this.

KENNY *falls asleep.*

BILBO. I turn the key. Frank says nothing. I make us tea with no milk. Frank says nothing. We have a Club Biscuit. Frank says nothing. We watch *Pet Rescue*. Frank says nothing. Then we turn the TV off. And Frank says:

FRANK. You know. Don't you?

*Beat.*

PEARL (*to* SHAUN). I want to be touched.

SHAUN. What?

PEARL. I want you to /

SHAUN. Don't.

PEARL. I want to know how it *feels* to /

SHAUN. Have you never /

PEARL. Course I fucking have, I'm twenty! But I wanna know
how it's *meant* to feel. I'm talking about *one* night, Shaun.
Tonight.

*Pause. They're close. Decisions.*

SHAUN. I'm sorry. I'm sorry. I can't.

PEARL *looks at him for a moment. Then she grabs her bag
from the bar and walks out.* SHAUN *hovers, winded, shaken.
He looks at* KENNY, *drooling.*

BILBO. Once Frank's tucked up I switch on the bar fire and
curl up on the sofa. But I can't sleep. There's so much to
*look* at. All the pictures and postcards and photos and doilies
and toy London buses and dried-out cactuses and china cats
and Russian dolls. Each little object with its own history.
Story. I try to imagine what they might be.

And I don't feel sad for him any more. For Frank.

I feel… jealous.

To have known such love.

PEARL *walks back into the pub, chucking her bag on the
bar as she does. She strides up to* SHAUN.

SHAUN. Oh, did you forget your /

*She kisses him. They kiss. For a long time. She pulls away.*

PEARL. Don't follow me, Shaun.

*She exists as swiftly as he entered, without looking back. He waits for a moment, sits, thinks. Looks to the audience. Goes to speak. Doesn't. Grabs his bag and leaves the pub.*

*A lighting change. Very early morning.* KENNY *begins to stir. He moans a little, especially when he lifts his head from the table. It pounds. He looks around. Tries to make sense of what has happened. He sees the broken cue. Confused. He gets up. His legs are weak. He looks and feels like shit. He staggers to the bar. Lets out a long moan. He gets behind the bar. Goes towards the cellar door. Leans out of it slightly.*

KENNY. BILL?

*The noise of his own shouting hurts too much. He finds an empty pint glass. Holds it up. Kisses it. Looks to the audience. Smiles.*

A drink in your hand;
your head in the sand.

*He puts it under the Foster's pump. Pulls it. Nothing.*

Fuck.

*Blackout.*

*End.*

**A Nick Hern Book**

*We Anchor in Hope* first published in Great Britain in 2019 as a paperback original by Nick Hern Books Limited, The Glasshouse, 49a Goldhawk Road, London W12 8QP, in association with W14 Productions and The Bunker

*We Anchor in Hope* copyright © 2019 Anna Jordan

Anna Jordan has asserted her moral right to be identified as the author of this work

Cover image design by Tom Scurr and David Ralf

Designed and typeset by Nick Hern Books, London
Printed in the UK by Mimeo Ltd, Huntingdon, Cambridgeshire PE29 6XX

A CIP catalogue record for this book is available from the British Library

ISBN 978 1 84842 903 1